Called to
LIVE

BILLY COLEMAN

MW00454713

ISBN 978-1-0980-9912-1 (paperback)
ISBN 978-1-0980-9914-5 (digital)

Copyright © 2021 by Billy Coleman

All rights reserved. No part of this publication may be reproduced, distributed, or transmitted in any form or by any means, including photocopying, recording, or other electronic or mechanical methods without the prior written permission of the publisher. For permission requests, solicit the publisher via the address below.

Christian Faith Publishing, Inc.
832 Park Avenue
Meadville, PA 16335
www.christianfaithpublishing.com

Printed in the United States of America

CONTENTS

Called to Live

CHAPTER ONE

Called to Live

And He died for all, that those who live
should live no longer for themselves, but for
Him who died for them and rose again.
—2 Corinthians 5:15

I made a commitment to accept Christ as my savior and to serve Him when I was very young. And while there were certainly strong emotions surrounding that commitment, it was just as much a practical decision that pointed my life in a certain direction. Here I am many years later, still going in that direction. Of course, there have been times when I have gotten offtrack for a while—where my priorities have gotten out of whack. But Christ has always been there, always close enough to keep me moving in His direction, regardless of how slow I might be going. His love has always been strong enough to pick me up and not allow me to quit. His grace is always enough to overcome my faults and failures. His forgiveness is always enough to deliver me from captivity. I'm not as close as I'd like to be, but I think I'm closer than I used to be, and that's something. He has provided purpose and strength the entire trip and a whole lot of joy and excitement.

I must admit, however, that there are and have been other loves in my life...like sports.

I have always loved all kinds of sports. When I was in high school, I participated in as many as I could, which were three. I played football in the fall, basketball in the winter, then came spring training football, then tennis in the spring, and then spring practice in basketball. Of course, during the summer, I practiced my sports as well as fished, and during the winter, my dad and I enjoyed hunting together. My parents quickly found that my love for sports was great insurance that I make good grades. Their expectations for me were very high, and all they had to do was mention, "No As, no play," and I was well on my way to the honor roll.

As a Christian, I found that sports provided an opportunity to witness for Christ. I wish I could say that spiritual goal was always foremost on my mind. Too often, the game took over first place, but sometimes He really used my life, and when He did and when He does, that is the ultimate victory. Coach Tom Calvin, my football coach and a legend in Alabama high school football, let me do a couple of devotions for our team when I was a senior. I was the chaplain of the Sylacauga High School letterman's club. I began speaking in churches when I was fifteen and preached my first sermon, if you could call it that, when I was sixteen. It was during this time that I began to think about what God wanted me to do with my life, what He was calling me to do.

After high school graduation, I went to the college of my dreams, a member of the powerful Southeastern Conference. And of course I would walk on and contribute to one of the sports teams, right? Well, sure. At 145 pounds soaking wet, I would certainly make a glorious addition to some varsity team. I first went and talked to the football coach. I had been told that I was very fast, but I found out that in the SEC, there were guys who were very fast who were also very big! And on top of that, they were very mean. I went to check out basketball practice, and to my dismay, SEC basketball players are very tall. Besides, at the practice I attended, two guys went after a loose ball in the stands, got into a fight, and one knocked the other's front two teeth out. My mom had spent a lot of money on me in high school for braces, so I felt "led" to go out for the tennis team. I practiced with the tennis team my freshman year and really enjoyed it. But like so many other times in my life, God's blessings would come through people. My decision to play tennis began a lifelong friendship with Reg, another walk-on, that never would have occurred otherwise.

College life was great. I was making good grades, things were going pretty well in tennis, and I got to go watch all the great sporting events. I was rooming with some of my closest friends from high school. My parents would come down on "football Saturdays," and in the South, it just doesn't get any better that that.

However, spiritually, there seemed to be an emptiness that to this day is very hard to describe. It's not that I was doing anything "wrong"; Christ was very much a part of my college experience. Because of Him, my love for sports, and the guidance of my parents, I had never been exposed to the kinds of temptations that many young people fall into. But sometimes I think we too often consider sin as things we do, maybe bad things. Many times, the sins of omission are the ones that slowly move us away from Christ. I just didn't think I was actively doing anything for Him. I was going through the motions of being a Christian, not really being His person.

Between studying and practicing tennis, I began reading the book *In His Steps*, a story about a group of people who decide to base all the decisions in their lives on the question, What would Jesus do? I was fascinated by the impact this decision had on their lives and felt that I needed to somehow respond to the emptiness I was feeling. I decided that I would take one year of my life, and to the best of my ability, I would try to make my every decision based on what I thought Christ would do.

To help hold myself accountable, I decided to keep a diary of each day's decisions. Each night, I recorded the events of the day. After the first couple of weeks, my list of decisions was not very impressive. "Today I was getting beat pretty bad in tennis. I decided that Jesus would not get mad." Or how about, "Today I decided to park farther away from class so someone else could have the closer parking place." I mean, those are certainly positive things, but something inside of me wondered if I was just playing a game with God. You know some of us are pretty good at that. On a Thursday night, I wrote, "In my heart, I believe that God is going to put me to the test. He is going to find out how serious I am about my commitment."

Friday morning I got my answer. The phone rang.

"Hello?"

"Yes, hello, is this Billy Coleman?"

"Yes, sir."

"Hey, Billy, this is Jack Edgar, district superintendent. How are you doing?"

"Fine, Dr. Edgar. I'm surprised to hear from you." I knew Dr. Edgar when I had been the youth pastor of a church in his district while I was I high school. He was a wonderful Christian man.

"Well, I'm a little surprised to be calling. Listen, we've got a church just south of Birmingham whose minister left three weeks before the end of the conference year, and we need someone to fill in these last few weekends. I thought of you. I know you do a lot of speaking, and I think you could really help us out. You could come up on Friday nights and go back after church on Sunday nights. Would you consider that? Hello... Billy?"

My silence lasted a few more seconds. It wasn't the request. I was more than willing to do that. After all, it was only three weekends. More than that, it was the awareness that God was active in my life and very much aware of the commitment I had made. God, the maker of the universe, was really interested and involved in my little insignificant life. I thought about what I had written the night before and thought, *Hey, I even have it on paper!*

What would Jesus do? I was excited. I know it was only for three weekends, but I was going to give it everything I had. I remember walking into the parsonage on that first Friday night. I mean, it was a whole house, with a kitchen and two bathrooms and everything! On Saturdays I would visit in the community and conduct the services on Sunday. The people at Mount Tabor United Methodist Church were great. They seemed excited that I was excited. It seemed that the last few years had been difficult at the church, and they were just glad to have me there. We had Sunday school, morning and evening services, and then I would go home. The three weeks flew by.

Then came the second phone call.

"Hello?"

"Billy, hey, Jack Edgar again. Listen, I've met with the pastor parish relations committee, and they want to know if you would consider being their pastor for the year. They feel God has led you to their church. Would you consider that? Hello, Billy?"

This time, the silence was longer. I mean, those three weekends were great, but wait a minute. All my life I had dreamed of attending this college. What about the tennis team? What about rooming with my friend Reg? What about having the family down to my apartment on "football Saturday"? These and other questions slowly disappeared, and only one question remained. What would Jesus do?

I was the pastor at Mount Tabor for four wonderful years. At nineteen, you are everybody's adopted son. Your faults and failures are overlooked, and your new mommas and daddies would fight to defend you. I was welcomed at everyone's breakfast table…and lunch and supper too, for that matter. We shared our lives together, even took vacations together. And through my imperfections, God used our love for Him and our love for one another to help our church grow and to help our spiritual lives to grow. I met my beautiful wife and her family there. I have lifelong friends at Mount Tabor and in the Westover community. I had to change colleges and didn't get to play sports, at least not in college. I did teach tennis lessons and played on a pretty mean church softball and basketball team. I commuted to school for four years but didn't mind it at all. My priorities had shifted. Life was forever changed, and my walk with Christ was growing. By the way, at the end of my yearlong commitment to "What would Jesus do?" I had to make an adjustment. You see, for a year, I picked up every hitchhiker I saw, and my mom was about to have a nervous breakdown. I look back and think that God was protecting me in my sincerity, but I did promise my mom that I would use more common sense. I regularly thank God for leading me in a decision that forever changed my life.

Through those great four years, I continued to search for God's call on my life. I felt strongly that He was leading me into a coaching and teaching ministry, and that is what I prepared for in college. In 1978, I graduated from college and prepared to take my first coaching job. Things had gone really well at Mount Tabor, and several good friends in the pastoral ministry thought I was really making a mistake. I still remember a friend whom I have great respect for saying, "Billy, you're crazy. You take your Christian philosophy into coaching and education, and they'll eat you alive. It's different out there in the world, you know. All they care about is winning."

My competitive juices started to flow. I thought, I know that it's different out there in the world. But Jesus is out there in the world, and He calls us to go out there in the world. And if He is with me and I am willing to work"—and I was willing to work very hard—"then I think I might just make it." And so a new chapter in my life began.

My first teaching and coaching job was at Benjamin Russell High School in Alexander City, Alabama. I got the job because of a contact I had through my time at Mount Tabor and because I was probably the only coach in the state of Alabama who was certified to teach speech. I had decided in college that I wanted to teach subjects in school that related to everyday living for young people. I hoped that I could inject my Christian philosophy more easily into those subjects. So I came out of college certified to teach speech, sociology, and health. I dearly love teaching all three subjects, and it was the speech endorsement that helped me land that all-important first job. Benjamin Russell needed a speech teacher and a coach. I was basically the only one available. God was working! Also, the head football coach at that time was Don Roberts, who became one of my closest Christian friends. At Benjamin Russell, I was the defensive coordinator in football, assistant basketball coach, and I started a boys' and girls' tennis team. I also taught five periods of speech.

My wife, Shireen, and I were married in July before I started work in August. The day after we returned from our honeymoon, I went to my first coaching clinic. From that day forward, it was long hours of work…lots of work…and then more work. Let there be no doubt that Shireen's "call to live" as a coach's wife required much more dedication than I could ever muster. We started the school's first Fellowship of Christian Athletes. I had the opportunity to speak in a lot of different churches. I even became the pastor at another church outside Alexander City for two and a half years, Friendship

United Methodist Church. It was a wonderful five years, and God's "call to live" was becoming clearer.

In every assistant coach's life, there is the dream of being a head coach one day. My dream was fulfilled in 1983, when I accepted the head football coaching position at West Point High School, a very large rural school in North Central Alabama. I was able to teach health and sociology and started another chapter of the Fellowship of Christian Athletes. Once again, I poured myself into a job, probably at the expense of family and everything else. By then, Shireen and I had two sons, Wesley (2) and Ryan (newly born). In fact, Ryan was born in transient between Benjamin Russell and West Point, but that's a story for another time. I have always been impressed how Shireen was able to work that little feat.

We were at West Point for three years and had a couple of pretty good football teams before I was offered the position of head football coach at Dora High School, north of Birmingham. Dora was playing really good football at that time. This was going to be a job with more pressure and higher expectations. Another friend advised me, "Billy, I think you ought to think twice about Dora. You know, your Christian philosophy is a perfect fit for West Point, but you are fixing to see the real world." Seems like I had heard those words before. Still, I had explained my philosophy during the interview, and they still offered me the job. I knew I was being led by God to do this. So Shireen, Wesley, Ryan, and I packed up and went to Dora. Well, mainly Shireen packed up because I was already working at Dora sixteen hours a day the summer before we actually moved. I was driven to work hard for a lot of reasons, some good, some not as good. Certainly, Christ was in the middle of all this, but there were other motives. I kind of wanted to prove some things. Okay, I really wanted to prove some things...to myself and to others. And I was going to work really hard to make it happen.

We spent three great years at Dora. We had very successful football teams. I was able to teach speech and sociology. We started a Fellowship of Christian Athletes. To the glory of God, Dora more than accepted the Christian philosophy I adhered to. I was getting to speak more than ever. You know a coach is a nondenominational kind of a guy, and I have had the pleasure of speaking at about every type of church there is. I have also been able to speak at a lot of special events such as youth rallies and Emmaus Walks, a three-day Christian retreat that has really been used by God to change lives.

We made lifelong friends at Dora, but I must admit that in those three years, God began to change me in some ways I needed changing. When I went to Dora, I just knew that Christ and I, or maybe I should say "I and Christ," were going to eventually coach the best football program in Alabama. Our success at Dora was going to either become "the dream job" or propel us to "the dream job," who knows, maybe into college coaching. But things were starting to change. I'm sure I was getting burned out, but more than that, Wesley and Ryan were growing up all too fast. And while they spent a lot of time at the field house, they were reaching the age where they need more time with me away from the field house. Shireen needed more than a husband who spent most of his hours and, more importantly, most of his energy away from home. God's "call to live" was moving me into new priorities.

In the spring of 1988, I spent one of the most humbling evenings of my life. A number of people from West Point, some friends and some new faces, came to our home and talked to us about returning to West Point. I was so overwhelmed by their presence that I didn't know how to respond. Their football coach the last three years, and one of my best friends, had resigned, and they were looking for a new coach.

I prayed a lot after they left, not just about the job but mostly about my life and the new direction I was being led into. Not that I wasn't excited about coaching at West Point; I was, and I knew I would continue to work as hard as I could. For the first time, I began to think about how many times Shireen and I had moved in our lives. It was time to find out where "home" was. West Point was a K-12 school, one of the few left in Alabama. Wesley and Ryan would be attending school, Shireen would be teaching fourth grade, and I would be teaching and coaching—all in the same place. Priorities were changing places. It was time to go "home."

I coached six years at West Point. We had some good teams, and during the last of those six years, we had West Point's only undefeated team in history. It was one of those "magical, once in a lifetime" years. Our Christian youth organization at school was really growing, and young people were finding Christ.

In 1994, the principal at West Point and a good friend of mine was elected superintendent of education for the Cullman county school system. West Point would be in need of a new principal. I had gotten my master's degree in administration. After praying about it, I applied, and on July 1, I became the principal at West Point School. I was very apprehensive at first. I loved coaching and teaching and really hated to give that up. And what had I gotten myself into anyway? At least in coaching, there is an opportunity to win every time you step on the field, but in administration, the rules seemed to change. I became familiar with the phrase "no win situation." It didn't take long for me to agree with my friend who had warned me about my Christian philosophy in the world. I said to myself, "Billy, you really are crazy. Lord, is this really what you are calling me to do?" I got my answer on Labor Day 1996.

Our family was spending Labor Day together at a lake about two hours south of West Point. About 7:00 a.m., the phone rang. It was Francis and Randall Jones, two very good friends who both worked at school. "Billy, the high school's on fire, and it's about to burn to the ground." I just couldn't believe my ears. It seems some young men I didn't even remember had gone on a rampage throughout the western side of the county. Two schools had been set on fire. One of those was West Point High School. As we rushed home, I tried to prepare myself for what I was about to see. My best efforts were not enough. The only thing left standing was the front archway where the main entrance was. TV stations were everywhere. As I walked through the parking lot filled with fire trucks and TV vans, I heard people saying, "Here comes the principal." With my eyes and mouth wide open, several microphones were in my face. Cameras were running. God gives to us what we need when we need it. I remember a strange peace coming over me, not because I requested it but because I needed it. God was there, and I knew that if I let Him, we could use this situation for His glory.

Today, West Point High School is a beautiful facility, more than we could have ever dreamed prior to the fire. As I write this sentence, I am still the principal. Wesley and Ryan are in college. I still love sports. West Point is our home.

Throughout my life, I, like you, have asked the questions, "Lord, what is it you want me to do? You know I love you, but what is it you want me to do? Maybe you could write it on that wall over there. I promise you I'll do it, but what is it you want me to do? Do you want me to coach? When we go two and eight, surely you don't want me to coach. Do you want me to be a principal? When the school burns down, surely you don't want me to be a principal. Do you want me to be a teacher? A minister? A motivational speaker? A writer? Lord, what do want me to do?"

Several years ago, I got my answer.

I had been asked to attend a special church service by some of my football players. Our speaker was a well-known Christian athlete who, of course, got my interest going. And on the fingers of this Christian athlete were two national championship rings, so suffice to say, he had my undivided attention.

He told a story about waking up one morning and feeling God's spirit stopping him right on the edge of the bed and speaking to Him in that still voice that we have all sensed on our spiritual journey.

"Tim, you're not doing what I want most," God said to him.

"But, Lord," Tim said, "I really don't understand. Every time I'm asked to speak for you, I do."

I moved closer to the edge of my seat. I always was ready to speak for God. This was getting interesting.

"But that's not what I want most," said the Lord.

"Lord, I'm confused," Tim said. "The other night when I was speaking for you, several young people came to the altar and accepted you. Many others came and rededicated their lives to you. Remember?"

"Yes, I remember," the Lord said. "But that's not what I want most."

Now I was on the edge of my seat. I prayed to God that He reveal to me the answer to the question I had asked so many times in my life.

"Lord," Tim said, "I don't know what to say. Please tell me. What is it that you want most?"

I almost fell out of the pew as I leaned forward into the silence that followed.

Finally, Tim said that the Lord told him, "WHAT I WANT MOST FROM YOU IS ALL OF YOU."

When God answered this young man's question, He answered mine. Since that day, I have never asked God what He wants me to do. And if I may be so bold, I think I know what He wants from all of us. He simply wants all of us. Everything we are, all our hopes, all our dreams; He wants all of us.

Now please don't get me wrong. Every day people are called to do specific things, to be in specific vocations. I praise God for those servants who are called into various areas of service. God certainly wants pastors, coaches, principals, and teachers. But what God wants more are pastors who are all His, coaches who are all His, principals who are all His, and teachers who are all His. And until we are all His, we will never truly understand all He calls us to be.

God calls each of us to live—to live for Him each day, in every moment of our lives. He calls us to live for Him in each opportunity for a relationship with another. He calls us to live for Him right now, right this second. And if we give Him all of ourselves this second, the next second will take care of itself. Occupations and vocations will secure themselves in His will for our lives.

Too often, we identify our lives with our occupations instead of with living for Him. Someone may come up to us and ask, "What do you do for a living?" We answer like, "I'm a teacher at the high school," or "I'm a mechanic over at the Ford place." Maybe in place of those answers, we should be saying, "I'm a Christian," or "I serve Jesus Christ for a living."

In my years of working with young people, I see something that greatly disturbs me. We adults seem to have given them the impression that you act one way when you're at church—you do and say things, you know, like Christians are supposed to—but when we get out into the world, that it's okay to act another way. Like at ball games or at parties, you don't have to really act like a Christian. And you can say cruel things to others in the world, things you would never say at church.

I forgot to tell you: I'm a *The Andy Griffith Show* fanatic. I'm a little worried that when I get to heaven, the Lord will say, "Billy, I notice that you know the dialogue from *The Andy Griffith Show* better than you know the scripture. Can you explain this?" Hopefully I won't say, "Lord, you, above all, should know what a great show it is." I hope you don't mind if I use a few examples from the show along the way.

There is one particular episode where Barney writes out a ticket for a guy named Fred Plummer for sweeping trash onto the street. Barney is shocked to find out that Fred is somewhat of a bully and takes offense to the ticket. He even goes as far as threatening Barney and tells him the first time he catches Barney out of uniform, "I'm gonna break every bone in your body."

Well, old Barn is scared to death and decides to never take off his uniform, which sends up red flags to Andy, who finally figures the whole thing out.

One day, Andy confronts Barney with the truth as only Andy can do.

"Barney, I've been thinking about this thing with you and Fred Plummer. I've been thinking about it a lot."

"You have?"

"Yes, I have. And you know what I think?"

"What?"

"I think you're gonna have to stand up to him. Barn, you're a symbol of the law. You and I both are symbols of the law. When people look at us, they don't just see Barney Fife and Andy Taylor. They see the law, and they ought to have respect for the law. You and I have worked awful hard for that respect, and I don't think we ought to give it up."

"Well, yeah, I agree with you on that, Ange."

"Yeah, and it's not something that should be tied to what we're wearing either. We should have it whether we're wearing our uniform or a salt-and-pepper suit. If it's something we put on when we get up in the morning and take off when we go to bed at night, then we got nothing. You see that, don't you, Barn? We're lawmen, no matter what we've got on."*

Being a Christian is a lot like that. If it's something we put on when we go to church and take off when we get back, then we got nothing. Our relationship with Christ is with us no matter where we are, no matter where we go. He calls us into the world to do a lot of things, but most of all, He calls us to give Him all of us and to live each moment for Him.

---

* *The Andy Griffith Show*

Relationships

CHAPTER 2

Relationships

Jesus entered Jericho and was passing through.
A man was there by the name of Zacchaeus; he
was a chief tax collector and was wealthy. He
wanted to see who Jesus was, but being a short
man he could not, because of the crowd. So
he ran ahead and climbed a sycamore-fig tree
to see him, since Jesus was coming that way.
When Jesus reached the spot, he looked
up and said to him, "Zacchaeus, come
down immediately. I must stay at your
house today." So he came down at
once and welcomed him gladly.
—Luke 19:1–6

We all have our favorite words: words that have special significance, words that make a difference in our lives. If I had to pick one, it would be the word *relationship*. I know if we put it to a vote, *relationship* would probably not win a favorite word contest, so let me take a moment to state my case.

If we indeed did take a vote, I dare say that *love* would probably be most people's favorite word. Now don't get me wrong. *Love* is a great word—one of the best! And in the life of a Christian, it is even more important. Paul said, "Three things remain: faith, hope, and love, but the greatest of these is love." Jesus said all the commandments could be condensed into two, and in each of those, we see the word *love*—loving God and loving our neighbor. Let there be no doubt that love is truly one of the secrets to the Christian life. But then again, I think of the love that my wife, Shireen, and I have for each other. Before that love was born, there first had to be a relationship. I remember when we first met. We talked and did things together. We got to know each other better in time. And it was out of that relationship that our love for each other began to grow. Love is born out of a relationship, and it is through that relationship that love reaches its fullest potential.

Many would say that the greatest word would be *faith*. And *faith* is a great word. With faith, we can "move mountains." But I would simply ask, "Faith in what? Faith in who?" There have been three different times in my life when I have stood in front of a new football team and introduced as the new football coach—a group of strange faces looking at a stranger face. Needless to say, this can be an awkward situation. In spite of my very best attempt to make a good impression, I must admit that there was probably very little faith present in those initial moments. I seriously doubt that those guys had very much faith in me, and honestly I probably did not have a lot of faith in them. But after that first meeting, something almost miraculous started to happen. We begin to work together, to spend time together. We share one another's joys and sorrows, one another's victories and defeats. We begin to share a relationship with one another, a deep relationship that crosses over the walls we spent years building to keep others out. And that group of strangers who met on that first day becomes a team, a unified group of individuals who share a relationship with one another. And out of those relationships, faith is born. Those players begin to believe in me as their coach; I begin to believe in each of them. Sometimes I think of those "pregame talks" we would have. There I would be looking out at our team with every player's eyes fixed on me, listening to every word I said—I mean really listening! In those moments, I would become overwhelmed with the responsibility I had been entrusted with. I thank God for the opportunities He has given me, and I have prayed for His strength on many occasions to live up to those responsibilities. Teams never become teams without faith, but first there has to be a relationship.

Many would say that the greatest word in the world is *Jesus Christ*. Christ is everything. He is the reason we live. He provides purpose and direction in our life. He gives us the strength to answer our call to live. But please hear me when I say that there are many in the world who know the word *Jesus Christ*, but they don't have a relationship with Him. And it is only until you have a personal relationship with Him that you really know who Jesus is and what He is about.

Relationship is a very important word, and our relationships are the foundations of our lives.

As a principal, I took the opportunity to teach one class each year. I love to teach, and no matter how things are going, this assured me of at least one hour of fun each day. Now that you know how I feel about relationships, I'm sure you may have guessed what I taught; that's right, sociology, the study of relationships! I got to preach every day; the students just didn't know it! We talked a lot about the importance of their relationships and that whether they come to school, happy or sad, was probably directly related to the conditions of their relationships. Friend to friend, parent to child, boyfriend to girlfriend: these are the factors that have an impact on a teenager's life. And quite frankly, if these relationships are in troubled waters, then it is very hard to get their attention at school. Most of us are like that. If we're not happy in our relationships, then we're not happy, and it seems that nothing else matters.

I guess we all have "things" that have special importance to our lives—those items we would get out first if the house were burning down. Let me share with you three of the most precious possessions in my life.

As I have already mentioned, I was the pastor at Mount Tabor United Methodist Church when I was in college. It was four of the greatest years of my life. We shared our lives together in a way that is hard to put into words. When it was time to graduate and move on to my first coaching and teaching job, let me tell you there was a lot of "wailing and gnashing of teeth." We had grown so close to one another. I thought my heart was going to break into a million pieces. When I left, the church presented me with a book that I will always cherish. Within the pages of that little book were letters that people in the church and the community had taken the time to write to me. I recently got that book out and reread those letters of love. Once again, I was touched by the relationships. Some of those letters were written by children who today have children of their own. I thank God that those relationships we have in Christ will never stop growing and will never end.

My second item is from when I coached at Dora High School. We had very good athletes to work with and a group of great coaches. There had been three successful seasons with the promise of more to come. But as I mentioned earlier, God was changing some priorities in my life and leading me in a different direction. At our end-of-the-year athletic banquet, the athletic department at Dora presented me with something I will never forget. It was a wood carving of the head of Christ, made with a chain saw: a remarkable work of art. The carved inscription read, "No greater love has any man than he would lay down his life for his brother." Many times I looked at this treasure and remembered what is really important and remember those wonderful relationships with young people and friends of that community. Many altars have used that sculpture of Christ during Emmaus weekend retreats and church services. I kept it in my office at school, so when West Point High School burned down, it was lost in the fire. A very close friend of mine replaced it a few years ago with an identical one, once again carved with a chain saw. When I look at it now in my office, I still think about the Dora community along with my good friend Rick.

In 1994, I was able to be a part of West Point's only undefeated football team in school history. Once again, the key to a successful season was present—very, very good players. At our football banquet that year, I was presented with a quilt, made by the parents and grandparents of our seniors. It is truly unbelievable. Around the outer edge of the quilt are football helmets, each with the interwoven name of a senior. I have it hanging in my office at West Point. Few visitors leave without mentioning the beauty of the quilt. When I look at it, I don't think about the wins—well, maybe a little. But more than the wins, I think about those special players who worked so hard to make a dream a reality. I think about the relationships.

Now some could easily say that it's only paper or just a piece of wood or a piece of cloth. But when the book, the wood, and the cloth become symbols of the relationships they represent, when the faces and lives of people become interwoven with your own life, then these objects or "things" become more precious than gold. Relationships change paper, wood, and fabric into eternal treasures.

A great deal of this book is about living for Christ through relationships. Relationships with friends and family are important in our lives. Building relationships with others is a powerful tool to be used by God. But what we must remember is that it is our relationship with Christ that is the foundation of who we are. If the word *relationship* is the most important word in the world, then the most important relationship in the world is our relationship with Christ.

When I was a freshman in college, I had the opportunity to have a professor who openly claimed to be an atheist. On the first day, Dr. Jones explained that if our beliefs were fragile and could not take the "scrutiny of logic and knowledge," then perhaps we should drop the class. Most of the students whom I knew to be Christians did drop the class, but I was intrigued. First of all, Dr. Jones was a great teacher, but mostly I think it was my competitive nature that made me stay. The weeks that followed were amazing. I had grown up in the church around Christians who always supported my belief system. I had never had anyone question my beliefs like they were questioned during those ten weeks. And on top of that, Dr. Jones could recite scripture better that than anyone I have ever known to this day! We argued every day in class. Sometimes I know the other students would roll their eyes when I would raise my hand to ask a question or comment, but I really think that on most days, they enjoyed our debates, if you could call them that. You see on most arguments, a judge would probably have said that I lost. Dr. Jones was the most intelligent man I have ever known, and try as I might, he won most of the time. I said *most* of the time: there was one argument I always won, and I think he knew it. One day, I came in and asked Dr. Jones how his weekend went. He said, "Good, brother. How was yours?" Dr. Jones always called us brother or sister, another one of his little ways of making fun of Christians.

I answered, "It went great. You know what I did?"

"What?"

"I went fishing with my dad," I said. "We caught a bunch of crappie. Then we grilled steaks after church yesterday. My dad sure knows how to cook a good steak. Do you know my dad, Dr. Jones?"

Dr. Jones's eyes twinkled. We had been down this road before. "No, brother, I don't. But then again, you already knew that."

"That's right," I said. "You don't know my dad. You've never met him. But I've known him all my life. I guess there's really nothing you can tell me about my dad, can you, Dr. Jones? After all, you don't know him. But I do. Just like you really can't tell me anything about Christ because you don't know Him, do you? But I do know Him."

Dr. Jones smiled and began class. Once again, he won most of the arguments. But there was one thing he could never beat me on. He didn't have a personal relationship with Christ, and I did. And Dr. Jones couldn't lecture me on something he knew nothing about. I loved his class, and I think he liked me. I would see him sometimes out of class. He always looked out of place. It seemed that underneath all that intelligence, there was no room for people: no room for relationships. He always seemed so lonely, so isolated.

When the class was over, I went up to thank him. It's funny; I had grown so much as a Christian while I was taking his class. He made me search for answers. My faith got stronger from the challenge. Most of all, I realize that there was one thing in life that no one could take from me, and that was my personal relationship with Jesus Christ. Everything else is a by-product of knowing Him.

"Thanks, Dr. Jones. I have really enjoyed your class. You know, I grew as much as a Christian taking your class as I have any other time in my life."

He winced a little. The last words Dr. Jones ever said to me were, "All I can say, brother, is go and sin no more."

A few years ago, someone brought something to Sunday school class: an article off the internet written by an atheist. The article was about bashing Christians in the public arena. The author? You guessed it…my Dr. Jones. Twenty years later, he was still doing it. Most of all, he still did not know what we know. I don't argue over spiritual things anymore. Thankfully, I've grown beyond that, but I still think of Dr. Jones and how my faith in Christ grew because of the challenges he presented to me. Most of all, I thank God for the one thing that no man can take away from me—a personal relationship with Jesus Christ.

One of the great stories about relationships in the Bible is the story of Zacchaeus. Remember the Bible school song:

> Zacchaeus was a wee little man and a wee little
> man was he
> He climbed up in the sycamore tree for the Lord
> he wanted to see
> And as the Savior passed his way, He looked up
> in the tree
> And He said, "Zacchaeus, you come down!
> For I'm going to your house for tea.
> I'm going to your house for tea"

Zacchaeus was not just your average sinner. Zacchaeus was a tax collector. And those were fighting words on the road to Jericho. Maybe it was something that Jesus said. Or maybe it was something that Jesus did. Anyway, Zacchaeus wanted to get a look at the man everyone was talking about. Being short of stature, he climbed up a sycamore tree so he could see Jesus, never realizing that he was in the tree so *Jesus could see him.* We can only imagine the look on Zacchaeus's face when Jesus looked right up in that tree and began to speak to him.

When I was about five, my parents took me to Montgomery to see my first rodeo. I don't remember a lot about it, but I do remember that Dennis Weaver, who played Chester on *Gunsmoke*, was the master of ceremonies. Chester was Marshall Dillon's famous deputy whose trademark was his walk with a limp. At the opening of the rodeo, a convertible drove around the arena with Chester perched up on the back of the car. He was waving to the crowd, acting like he was really glad to be there. I loved watching *Gunsmoke*, and Chester was somewhat of a legend to me. As the car passed by, I stood as high as my tiptoes would allow and waved to one of my heroes. All of a sudden, Chester stood up in the back seat, took off his cowboy hat, looked right at me, and said, "Hey, partner!" I was stunned. I quickly sat down and looked around. There were a lot of people in the stands. We were several rows up. Is it possible that Chester was looking and talking to me? I glanced over at my parents. "I believe he was talking to you, son," my dad said.

Wow, I thought. *Talk about cool. Chester looked right up at me and said, "Hey." All those people and he looked at me.*

Do you think that's what Zacchaeus thought? *All these people around and Jesus is looking at me.* Zacchaeus climbed the tree to look at Jesus, but here Jesus was looking at him. He'd seen important people before and noticed how their looks would pass right over him, like he wasn't even there. But this person was different. He was looking right at him, like he *wanted* to see him.

"Zacchaeus, come down. I'm going to stay at your house today."

Zacchaeus probably looked at the guy in the tree beside him and said, "Is He talking to *me?*"

The guy in the tree probably asked, "Is He talking to *you?*"

Peter probably said, "Say what?"

The Pharisees said, "The man has gone to be a guest of a sinner."

But Matthew probably only smiled. Being a fellow tax collector, he understood.

You see, Jesus wanted to have a personal, individual relationship with Zacchaeus. He wants to have a relationship with all of us. Of all the people in the crowd, of all the people in the world, He wants to have a relationship with me! He actually wants to know me personally. He wants to go home with me; He wants to stay with me! The creator of this world wants to have a relationship with me through His Son Jesus Christ! And He wants to have one with you!

Jesus did go home with Zacchaeus that day, with that sinful tax collector! And a while later, Jesus said, "Today salvation has come to this house." And Zacchaeus was never the same again, and neither are we. Zacchaeus had a personal relationship with Christ. So do we.

Jesus was always reaching out, always wanting to build relationships. He walked through a large crowd, stopped, and said, "Who touched me?"

"Master," the disciples said, "all these people and you ask that question."

But He looked, and He looked until He found the woman who had been sick for twelve long years. And He healed her.

A woman caught in the act of adultery, two fishermen in a boat without a fish all day, a thief on a nearby cross: Jesus Christ always had the time. And He wants to have a personal relationship with each one of us. It does not matter who we are or where we have been—in a crowd or up a tree, He wants to go home and abide with us.

As we answer the call to live for Christ, He will use our relationships to change the world. One of my favorite stories is about a young Hindu girl who enrolled into a Christian college. Well, she was fair game for every Christian around, and pretty soon there emerged a sort of competition to see who would lead the young lady to Christ. Many shared their personal stories of faith with her. Many read great Bible scriptures to her. Many others prayed for her.

Finally, one morning at a chapel service, this young girl came down to the front and accepted Jesus Christ as her savior. At the end of the service, the minister presiding asked her to please share who it was or what it was that brought her to Christ.

In broken English, she began to share, "First of all, I want to thank all of you for what you have done for me. I know many of you have been praying for me. I really appreciate all the sharing you have done with me. Thank you so much. All these things have meant so much to me. But you know, when I really think about it, what really brought me to Christ was my roommate. We would go places together and do things together. We shared each other's time and each other's lives. Me and my roommate, we had a friendship, *and in that friendship, Jesus built a bridge from her heart to mine and just walked over.*"

What a great message! What a great opportunity! Jesus Christ is our greatest relationship, and He uses relationships to make His presence known in the lives of others.

> Me and my roommate, we had a friendship,
> and in that friendship, Jesus built a bridge from
>   her heart to mine
> and just walked over.

The Better Way

CHAPTER 3

————⊷⟨⟨⟩⟩⊶————

The Better Way

As Jesus and His disciples were on their way,
He came to a village where a woman named
Martha opened her home to him. She had a
sister named Mary, who sat at the Lord's feet,
listening to what He said. But Martha was
distracted by all the preparations that had to
be made. She came to Him and asked, "Lord,
don't you care that my sister has left me to do
the work by myself? Tell her to help me!"
"Martha, Martha," the Lord answered, "you are
worried and upset about many things, but only
one thing is needed. Mary has chosen what is
better, and it will not be taken away from her."
—Luke 10:38–42

When I was a teenager, some leaders in my hometown became convinced the community needed to do something for the youth—
provide some activities and places to go on weekends. It's a common theme that has frequented many towns and cities in America.
Sylacauga, Alabama, was a great place to live in 1972, but like many
small towns, there wasn't a whole lot for teenagers to do on Friday
and Saturday nights, at least not of the positive variety. A "Bridge
over Troubled Waters" committee was set up to address the problem.

I was selected to be the representative from the high school with my pastor, John Mann. God used Brother Mann to make a powerful impact on my life. Several of us on that committee believed that we needed a Christian place, a sort of hangout, in town where young people could go to socialize, be involved in various programs, and find spiritual opportunities if desired. We found the perfect building, close to the local pizza place and in the middle of town. As we began to plan the details of our new Christian youth center, the first order of business was to come up with a name. After much prayer and discussion, we decided on The Better Way, and before long, we were open for business! Although I didn't realize it then, now almost thirty years later, I think about what a great name that is: good enough to name a chapter after it, good enough to describe one of the great scriptures of the Bible.

The story of Mary and Martha has powerfully impacted my life and the way I look at my relationship with Christ. It has probably brought about more change in my own spirituality than any other scripture I can think of. Let's take a closer look.

"Jesus is coming to my house today!" That surely must be what Martha thought and said to her friends when she found out about the Lord's visit. "Did you hear? Jesus is coming to my house. Oh, yes, He said so Himself. We're really good friends, you know. It's going to be a special day. Everything is going to be perfect!"

Try to imagine Martha's excitement. Of course, there was a lot to do. The house had to be cleaned as never before. All of Jesus's favorite dishes had to be prepared, and there had to be plenty of it too. Those disciples of His were big eaters, and along with them, many other special guests would be invited. Extra seating had to be borrowed from the neighbors. There had to be room for everyone when the Master started telling His stories...well, there was just a lot to do. Everything did have to be perfect, and maybe that was where the problem began.

Martha had anticipated a lot of help from her sister Mary, and she had been a big help, at least until Jesus arrived. As soon as He entered, Mary was drawn to Him, and soon she was sitting at His feet, gazing into His eyes, listening to His every word. Martha, on the other hand, was frantically running around the house, trying to get things done. She had glanced over at Mary a couple of times, trying to get her attention. After all, there was still a lot to do! Finally, Martha had taken just about all she could take. She went over to Jesus and said, "Master, don't you care that my sister has left me to do the work by myself?"

Jesus looked into Martha's eyes, and when He did, He looked into mine. His response to her became His response to me. "Martha, Martha, you are worried and upset about many things, but only one thing is needed. Mary has chosen what is better, and it will not be taken away from her."

Busyness! Things to do! Places to go! Deadlines to meet! Schedules to keep! These are phases that become more than words; they become our lives. We frantically run from place to place. We don't jog; we sprint! And when we can't keep the schedule, when we can't meet the deadlines, when we're overwhelmed with the busyness of our lives, well, then we worry. We worry about things we can change, and we worry about things we can't change. We are "worried and upset about many things." That was the life of Martha, that has been the life of Billy Coleman, and perhaps that describes your life as well. It is important that we discover "the better way."

First of all, we need to remember that Martha was doing "good" things. She was serving, serving on the behalf of Jesus, in honor of Him being a guest in her house. We are badly mistaken if we think that she did not love Jesus just as much as Mary did. She had the best of intentions. Martha simply showed her love for Christ through gifts of service. However, there is a great trap that Martha and the rest of us often step into. Notice how the Bible says that Martha became "distracted" by all the preparations.

Distractions are priorities that cause us to lose focus on that which is most important. When someone visits a friend or neighbor, it is to spend time with that person and get to know them better, to deepen the relationship. Certainly, when Jesus visited Martha, the most important thing was to spend quality time with her and to grow in His relationship with her. Even though Martha busied herself with "good" things, they became distractions in her life. There was something more important—a better way.

We've all been exactly where Martha was, both literally and spiritually. Have you ever had company at your house, but you were so busy doing things, things that needed to be done, that you said, "Well, it doesn't seem we got to visit much, did we?" or "Maybe you can come again when we can just sit down and talk. I barely had time to say hello." In all the preparation, we lose focus of the real reason for the visit.

Even worse, it happens in our spiritual lives. We teach Sunday school. We sing in the choir. We go to all the services. We're on all the committees. We "do" all the right things, but maybe we're missing out on the most important thing. Is it possible to be so busy doing things for God that we don't have time for God?

I remember the first Fellowship of Christian Athletes meeting we had at my first coaching job. We invited the students to a recreation center with a swimming pool and plenty to eat. We had a huge crowd, and everyone was having a great time. Our first meeting was a big success. After a short devotional and prayer, we continued with the fellowship. It wasn't long before two of our very best football players walked up to me and said, "Coach, is this what you wanted?"

"Yeah, this is great, isn't it?" Then I looked at them more closely and said, "What do you mean?"

"I don't know," Sammy said, who later played linebacker at Georgia Tech. "I just wondered if this was what we wanted."

This time, I knew what he meant. We got everyone back together and had a real devotional with a lot of sharing about what our group was going to be about and how growing closer to Christ was to be our top priority. It's amazing how distracted we can become even with the best of intentions.

As an educator for twenty-five years, I have witnessed the phenomenon called "teacher" burnout. Young teachers enter their career on fire to make a difference in the lives of young people. For a few years, they can't do enough. They arrive at school early, and they leave late. They take work home. They eat, drink, and sleep school. After a few years, things begin to change. Feeling very little appreciation and with a mountain of paperwork staring them between the eyes, teachers begin to doubt those initial feelings of excitement. They begin to notice the toll their commitment has taken on their family and other aspects of their lives. They're tired, they're discouraged, and it seems nobody cares. Too often these wonderful teachers end their careers full of resentfulness and frustration. They become the last to get to school and the first to leave…teacher burnout.

Christians can be burned out too. I know. There was a time in my life when my Christian approach to living resembled my coaching philosophy, which was that I would simply outwork everyone else. If our team practiced longer and worked harder than anyone else, then we would be successful. As a Christian, I spoke everywhere I could, I taught everything I could, I sponsored every Christian youth group I could. There's a lot of "I" in that kind of Christianity, and pretty soon, "I" was burned out. I needed to sit at Jesus's feet. It was there I found "the better way," and it has made all the difference.

"Mary has chosen what is better, and it will not be taken away from her." Those were Jesus's words. While Martha was distracted by all the preparation, Mary certainly was not. There she sat at the feet of Christ, listening to Him, watching Him, spending time with Him. Exactly what was it that Mary had chosen that was better than what Martha was doing? Mary had chosen her relationship with Christ as her top priority, the most important thing in her life. Not that serving was not important. It certainly was and is. It's just that knowing Christ is more important. And knowing Christ strengthens us to be servants that we could never be on our own. It is through our relationship with Christ that we are empowered to be His person in the world. The channel of love and power He provides to us must be open if we are to make a difference. When we cut off our time with God, even though we are serving Him, we cut off the very source of strength we need to serve Him.

For centuries, the church has debated "grace versus works." Prior to Christ, we called it the law. The devout Jews followed the law with utter devotion, to the point that the law became an end within itself, not the means to harmonious living it was meant to be. The Pharisees cried "foul" when Jesus healed on the Sabbath, but Jesus saw into their hearts. That's the thing; the law deals with the outside actions of our lives, but it doesn't change our hearts. Jesus knew the problem with the law when he told the Pharisees, "You strain at a gnat and swallow a camel." While they focused on the outside, they had a much bigger problem on the inside—a heart problem.

The rich young ruler found out the futility of basing his faith on adhering to the law. "I've kept all of these," he said, referring to the commandments.

But he walked away from Jesus when he saw that his philosophy meant that he had to be perfect. In fact, Jesus told his disciples that it's impossible for those like this man to enter the kingdom of heaven. "Then who can be saved?" they asked. Jesus answered, "Humanly speaking, no one, but with God, all things are possible." There is a better way.

Since the early beginnings of the church, the concept of good works has been discussed. It seems to have replaced the law. Certainly, there can be no argument as to the importance of good works. "Faith without works is dead" (James 2: 17), and Jesus causing the fig tree to wither because it had no fruit are strong indications that our faith is called to action. Once again, let us be reminded that Martha was doing "good works" out of her love for Jesus.

On the other hand, there are those who remind us about 1 Corinthians 13:3: "If I give all I have to the poor and I am burned alive for preaching the gospel, but have not love, I gain nothing." Or "It is by grace you have been saved…not by works, lest any man should boast" (Ephesians 2:8–10). We are taught that you can't earn your way to heaven with good works. Simply put, grace means you don't earn it. It is freely given to you.

I think the real question to the Mary and Martha dilemma is not which one was right and which one is wrong. The real question is which is more important. Jesus told Martha, "Only one thing is needed. Mary has chosen what is better, and it will not be taken away from her." The bottom line is we are called to get close to Christ, to give Him all of us, and everything else will take care of itself. We can serve Christ on our own for a while with our good works, but sooner or later, we get burned out because we are relying on our own strength. In contrast, when we grow close to Christ and rely on Him, we allow His strength to work through us. There will be serving, and there will be plenty of good works, only it will be Christ through us, and "we can do all things through Christ, who strengthens us" (Philippians 4:13).

In chapter 2, we look at the story of Zacchaeus, how Jesus called him down out of the sycamore tree to go home with him. A relationship between Jesus and Zacchaeus was born. And as they spend time together, something powerful began to happen: Zacchaeus began to change. The immediate by-product of that change was that Zacchaeus wanted to serve. Listen to his response to Christ: "Look, Lord! Here and now I give half of my possessions to the poor, and if I have cheated anybody out of anything, I will pay back four times the amount" (Luke 19:8). Sounds like a man who wants to serve Christ with all his heart. Christian service is the natural response that emerges out of our personal relationship with Christ. He gives us the desire and the strength to be His servants in the world.

Several years ago, we had a girl at school who had everything going for her: well, almost everything. Sherry was beautiful, popular, and smart. She had a great personality and was liked by everyone. Her life was one accomplishment after another. There was only one thing, one thing that kept her from being complete. She was not a Christian. I had Sherry in my speech class that year, and she was a model student. She knew and respected my Christian views, and on more than one occasion, I had the opportunity to share some things with her about being a Christian. Our Warriors for Christ group sponsored a big youth rally in our gym that year. We had some wonderful guests who shared powerful testimonies about their relationships with Christ. To our delight, the gym was packed with young people from all over the county, and especially from our school, West Point High. At the close of the service, over 250 young people answered a call to accept Jesus Christ into their lives. That night, one week before her graduation, with knees firmly planted on the hard surface of a basketball court, a beautiful young lady named Sherry made her life complete by filling the void in her heart with Christ. Her faced shone with the light of Christ. As I shared with her this precious moment of joy, I couldn't help but think the difference in the world God would make through His new servant.

The next day, there was electricity in the air, except in this instance, the electricity was the Holy Spirit. Young people were sharing their faith with other students during class and in the halls. One young person came up to me at break and said, "Guess what, Coach Coleman, I accepted Christ."

"That's great," I said. "I didn't see you at the service last night."

"No, not last night," he answered. "I just accepted Him in biology class!"

I was teaching sociology during third period that day when there was a knock at the door. It was Sherry. "Coach Coleman, can I talk to you for a minute."

"Sure." I stepped outside in the hall and immediately noticed something wrong.

Sherry continued, "I don't know if you know this, but I have a boyfriend."

"Well, I guess I have to say that I'm not surprised."

As she looked away from me and focused on something down the hall, tears began flowing down her cheeks. "Coach Coleman, I respect you so much…this is hard to say." The silence only deepened. Finally, she said, "Last night, I accepted Christ, but…but, well, I just don't know if I can give up the sexual choices that I've been making. I'm scared. I don't know what to do. I don't know if I'm strong enough."

Few times in my life have I witnessed such sincerity and honesty. As He does with all of us, God was leading her to make changes in her life to deal with the sin of her past. I silently prayed that God give me the words to say to this young girl at such a critical time in her life. "I know you are worried about it, but don't. There is one thing and one thing only that you need to focus on. Get as close as you can to Christ. Each day, get close and stay close to Him. I believe if you do that, everything else will take care of itself. He will give you the strength and the desire to change. It's all about knowing Him."

Sherry graduated one week later, and I did not see her for two years. When I did finally did see her at "let's pray for our school night," an annual event at West Point the day before the opening of school each year, she was on fire for God. She had truly knelt at Jesus's feet. She had chosen the better way, and she was making a difference through Him.

Knowing Christ and focusing on Him makes all the difference in our lives. I recall the words of a song we learned at Promise Keepers:

> Knowing You, Jesus, knowing You
> There is no greater thing.

Or another song we sing at Fellowship of Christian Athlete Conferences:

> Just to be close to You is where I want to be
> Let me hide myself inside your heart to find my
> destiny
> Every step I take is one less step I need
> To be in your presence and close to You

I have been teaching a Bible study at our church for several years. I remember when I was first asked to lead it, I probably said yes as much out of obligation as anything else. I've never been good at saying no, and certainly not saying "no" to a Bible study. Don't get me wrong. In many ways, I wanted to do it, and I certainly needed it in my own life. It's just that "I was worried and upset about many things," just like Martha. I was coaching and teaching and involved in about a thousand other commitments. I was just too busy. The Bible study had been going for about a year, and things were going pretty good, I guess. Relying on the self-discipline of athletics, I made myself fulfill my responsibilities as teacher. Of course, I was doing it all on my own and pretty much running on an empty tank. One night, we were studying about the Holy Spirit and about what happens to worship services when Christians seek the presence of Christ. We collectively decided to ask the Holy Spirit to be a part of our little Bible study, and it has never been the same since, at least it has not for me. We pray for His presence each Wednesday night and ask that God remove the many distractions in our lives that keep our focus off Him. We have decided to spend some time at the feet of Christ, to get closer to Him. For me, it has made all the difference. My feelings of obligation have turned into the joy of opportunity. I eagerly anticipate each worship service. I used to plan the Bible study around my other responsibilities. Now I plan everything else around our Bible study; a team of wild horses couldn't keep me away.

Spiritual desire results when "keeping the law" is replaced with "the power of Christ." When we are close to Christ, growing in His spirit changes us from the inside out. "Having to" gives way to "wanting to." Serving becomes the natural by-product of knowing Him.

It's amazing how closeness to Christ changes your priorities. I am not sure we consciously change them; they just kind of change naturally. Things that you used to think were important suddenly are not that important anymore. Still other things become more important to you than you could ever imagine.

As a coach or as a player, it's hard to beat a locker room after a big win. Everyone is so excited about reaching a goal that you've really worked hard for. I've been blessed to be a part of some of those locker rooms. I thank God for the opportunity to have been able to stand in front a group of guys who are enjoying one of the high moments of life. It is wonderful to be able to look into their eyes and, in my joy and excitement, to be able to say, "Hey, guys, this is truly a great feeling, one of the best, but you know what, knowing Jesus Christ is even better." I thank God for being able to say that and mean it. For you see, I've been Martha, and I've been Mary. I have distracted myself with many "things," and I've sat at Jesus's feet, striving to get closer to Him. And as you have probable guessed, knowing Christ is the better way.

Emptied to Be Filled

CHAPTER 4

Emptied to Be Filled

> He must increase, but I must decrease.
> —John 3:30 (KJV)

When Becky stuck her head in the door of my office and said, "Mr. Coleman, can I see you for a minute," I knew something was wrong. One reason I enjoy working with teenagers so much is because they are honest with what they are feeling and much easier to read than older folks. We adults have spent years building our walls of isolation, sometimes to the point of making it impossible for someone to break through. We don't want anyone to know what we are really feeling. We are experts at playing the games of life, while teenagers are still in the novice stage. I think young people still cling to the hope that someone out there will listen and maybe help them find direction and purpose in life. Teachers, coaches, and principals have a wonderful opportunity to make that difference, to be that listener. Too often, however, we allow the world's busy schedule to distract us from what's really important.

As soon as she walked in the room and I shut the door, the walls came crashing down. She immediately began to sob and tried to explain, "I just don't know what's happening to my life. Everything seems to be falling apart. My parents are fighting all the time. I think they may be getting a divorce. I'm doing terrible in my classes. It doesn't seem like I have any friends. I feel alone. Mr. Coleman, I just don't know what to do."

After a short silence and before I could respond, Becky looked up and said, "You know, I'm a Christian. I've been going to church ever since I was saved a few years ago." While young people may be much easier to read, let me add that they are experts at reading others. Becky already knew what was going through my mind.

"Let's talk about what you said about feeling alone," I said. "Why did you become a Christian?"

"I wanted to become saved."

"Saved from what?"

She thought for a minute and said, "Saved from hell. I want to go to heaven."

"Becky, you know the really neat thing about being a Christian is that Jesus not only wants us to accept Him as our Savior, He want to live in us. He died for you so you can be forgiven of your sins, but three days later, He was resurrected so He could live in you. Going to heaven is great, but God wants to live in your life every moment. When He lives in us, we are never alone. Now the circumstances in our lives may or may not change, but He will always be with us. Becky, He wants to live in your life…right now."

Becky was listening. I figured it was time for me to keep my mouth shut and let God do the rest of the talking. We looked at some scriptures about Christ wanting to live in us from the gospel of John. We said a prayer, and in the next few weeks, I began to notice a change in Becky. We talked several more times during the course of the year. Her parents did get a divorce, but it was evident that Christ was living in her, and through her situation, He was using her life to touch others.

I once read a quote from Billy Graham that stopped me right in my tracks. I have mentioned this quote several times when I have spoken to different groups, and it almost always gets comments or questions. Dr. Graham said that a very high percentage of Christians in America today live defeated lives. Now when some people say something, it may go in one ear and out the other. But when Billy Graham says something, people listen. It certainly got my attention.

I think perhaps that God was speaking very powerfully through Dr. Graham when he made that statement. Too often, the world sees no difference between the life of a Christian and the life of a nonbeliever. The problem goes all the way back to Adam.

In the beginning, God had union with man. Man's eyes were closed to evil. There was only God, and man's relationship with God was everything. Unfortunately, man chose to disobey God, the result of which was sin, and sin became the barrier between the two. The relationship was replaced with "keeping the law." Man's failure to "keep the law" has been well-documented and reminds us of the impossibility of man's efforts to reach God. Yet it is not impossible for God to reach man, and with the coming of Jesus Christ, the opportunity for the relationship was reestablished. Salvation comes when we accept Christ as our Savior, but salvation is only the first step. Our sins are washed away; the barrier is removed! The stage is set for God to enter into our lives—to live in us through Christ. Christ died for us not just to ensure us of heaven, not just to give us victory over physical death, but Christ died for us and was resurrected so He can live in us—right now! In Christ, we have more than victory over death; we have a new way to live life! "Therefore if anyone is in Christ, he is a new creation; the old is gone, the new has come!" (2 Corinthians 5:17).

Too many times, we think that accepting Christ is all there is to it. We go through the motions of attending church, saying and doing all the right things on Sunday, but we don't allow Christ to fill us, to enter our lives on Monday through Saturday. We need His presence on our jobs, in our hobbies, in our homes, and on our vacations. We need His presence in the midst of our temptations, when we are losing the game, after we lost, and when we are winning. We need Him before we make our excuses, before we say a hurtful thing, before we think a hurtful thought. We need Christ in our lives before we blame someone else for our problems, before we criticize the referee, or before we pass by someone in need. We need Him in our lives when we see someone sitting alone in the lunchroom or when we see the obvious pain in a stranger's eyes. We need Christ in our lives when someone dislikes us, says something about us, or holds a grudge against us. We need Christ in our lives when our children turn to us for guidance, when our spouse needs unconditional love, or when our neighbor needs an example to follow. We need Christ when we see the hungry or the needy or the afraid. We need Christ in our lives when we make a mistake, when we fail, or when we need forgiveness. We need Him in our lives when we're searching for direction or purpose or strength. Being a Christian is more than knowing you have eternal salvation. Jesus Christ died for you so He can live in you. We need Christ in our lives right now, right this very moment. And not until He lives in us will we experience the total victory.

I have had the privilege of being able to coach some very good football players. Some were big and strong. Others were fast. Some had great hands. Many were very smart. A few were pretty mean… on the field, of course. I could spend a long time talking about guys who scored a lot of touchdowns, ran or passed for a lot of yardage, or who made a lot of tackles. While I certainly respect those outstanding abilities, the ones I want to talk about now are the players that I respected the most. Every team has and needs players like these, and I'm not so sure that, in the end, they don't get the most out of the game.

I'm talking about players who come to every practice, run every sprint, punish their bodies, make great sacrifices of their time, and then *don't get to play*. Every day they give their greatest effort, but because they don't have as much ability as another player, they don't get as much playing time on the field. These players I mention stand on the sidelines on Friday night and cheer for another guy who is playing the position they would like to play. Not only do their cheer for that player, they sincerely want him to be successful, even though a lack of success might get them into the game. I love these players because they are selfless. They are team players; team goals are more important to them than individual goals. It is this unselfishness that is going to make them successful in life. These players will go on to put family, others, and most of all, God ahead of self.

I know it's hard to believe that this is possible when you see our world today. We look at sports in the media and see almost nothing but selfishness, higher contracts, and playing time. The word *I* has taken the spotlight. Somehow, these unique players I have described have resisted the temptation to put self first. They have sat at the dinner table and heard family members say, "Why doesn't the coach play you more, son?" They have heard friends say, "Why don't you just quit? You never get to play." Yet they come to practice every day and give their best; they always put the team first. They cry when the team loses, and they celebrate when the team wins. The world doesn't understand their reasoning, but I promise you that the team understands and respects their actions. I tell you that I love them. They are winners in the highest sense of the word, and I have never coached a successful team without players like these.

John the Baptist was a team player.

With a great following and loyal disciples, John the Baptist had quite a ministry. His dedication was respected by many, even by those who did not believe. Although John's message clearly reflected his relationship to Christ, there were those who saw Jesus as a threat to his ministry. In the third chapter of John, several of John's disciples came to him and said, "Rabbi, that man who was with you on the other side of the Jordan—the one you testified about—well, he is baptizing, and everyone is going to him." John replies that he himself is not the Christ but that Jesus is. Furthermore, John says, "The bride belongs to the bridegroom. The friend who attends the bridegroom waits and listens for him and is full of joy when he hears the bridegroom's voice."

Then John says what I guess is my favorite verse of scripture in the Bible. "He must increase, but I must decrease." The New International Bible says, "He must become greater; I must become less." Regardless of what translation we choose, this scripture is the simplest, truest directive for me as a Christian. Christ is to increase in our lives, and we are to decrease. It's the goal of every day in our Christian life until He fills our lives and we are no more. As for me, I'm certainly not there yet. I think I am more of His than I used to be, but I'm not as much of His as I am going to be. It's a lifelong process of growing in Christ until He fills our life and overflows into the world.

One of my favorite illustrations when I'm talking to a group is to illustrate Christ filling our lives like water fills a jar. I take a large glass bowl, which represents the world, and place a quart-size jar inside it. The jar represents our lives in the world. Using a large pitcher of water, I begin to fill the jar. We talk about how Christ wants to fill our lives with his presence. Pretty soon, the jar becomes full, and water begins to run over the top of the jar into the bowl. Pretty soon the bowl also begins to fill with water. As I continue to pour, something amazing begins to happen. As the water begins to fill the bowl, the jar begins to disappear to those looking from the front. Standing over the top, I can see the jar sitting inside the bowl, but those in the audience cannot. The lesson is that fruit or "good works" is simply the overflow of God's spirit in our lives. It's really nothing we do, but as Christ begins to fill us, He overflows into the world. Also, as Christ begins to flow into the world around us, we start to disappear. The world doesn't see us anymore, only Christ's presence. As an empty vessel, we simply allow Him to fill our lives and flow into our world. Fruit is produced through us, not by us.

It's a neat illustration, but lately I've been thinking that maybe something is missing. It goes back to what John the Baptist said, "He must increase, but I must decrease." There are two things that are described in this scripture. First, there is the increasing importance of Christ in our lives. But second, and just as important, there is the decreasing importance of ourselves. The assumption has been that we are empty, in need of filling. But what if we are not empty, but simply *filled with the wrong things.* What if the problem is that Christ cannot enter our lives because we are too full of something else? Maybe my illustration would be better if my jar was full of sand, and let's say that the sand represented me. It would be necessary to empty the sand to make room for the water. Perhaps I must empty my life of self to make room for Christ's presence...two things, not one. "Christ must increase, but I must decrease."

Paul spends a lot of time talking about dying to self so we can live in Christ. To the Galatians, he writes, "I have been crucified with Christ and I no longer live, but Christ lives in me" (Galatians 2:20). To the church at Corinth, he says, "For we who are alive are always being given over to death for Jesus' sake, so that His life may be revealed in our mortal body" (2 Corinthians 4:11). Too often, we see sin as acts or situations in the world. The real problem is our sinful nature, and it must be changed from the inside through Christ living in us.

It's ironic how we promote self in today's society. We talk about getting in touch with ourselves; we go to self-help seminars where we are told about all the wonderful potential we have and how we can, through our own power, overcome all the obstacles in our lives. We are told to list all our good qualities and to recognize the potential we have to be successful in our life. Quite the opposite, Paul talks about how we must die to self, how we have to overcome our sinful nature through Christ, and how He can change our lives from the inside out. These philosophies seem to be total opposites.

When it comes to wheeling and dealing, let it be known that I am the sucker of the world. I'm the guy who lights up every salesman's face when they see me coming down the street. *That's the guy,* they think. They stand in line to approach me about new products that have come out or the vacation of a lifetime. I've always been that way. People can sell me things I can't give away. If someone says they want to sell something for twenty-five dollars, I say, "Would you take fifty for it?" Shireen does not allow me to go to sales of any kind. I'm not supposed to talk to salesmen on the phone either. But I'll tell you a secret. Sometimes, when she's not home, I talk to them, just a little. But I don't buy anything. I've learned that when it comes to buying and selling, I have no talent.

But let me tell you about a deal that even I could not blow. When Jesus Christ died for me on the cross, we made an exchange. He exchanged His body and blood, His righteousness and goodness, all He is. He exchanged all that for my sins, my faults, and my failures. It's a once-in-a-lifetime deal, and there's nothing fair about it. It is called grace, and it took the place of my sin. And as I decrease, as I empty myself, He increases in my life.

Emptying to be filled with Christ has a powerful effect in the believer's life. We think of those disciples—Peter, James, and John—whom Jesus took with Him that night into Gethsemane. In His most

49

needful hour, what did they do? They went to sleep. It doesn't sound like a group that would change the world. They were weak and full of self. But in Acts, we see these same men in a different light. The Holy Spirit has filled their lives, and they allow the power of Christ to act through them. And in the end, they are not asleep. They are fed to lions, skinned alive, and burned at the stake. But Christ had exchanged His power and grace for their sins and failures. And He continues to use their lives today for His glory.

When I went to interview for the head football coaching position at Dora High School, I had some apprehensions. I felt confident about the coaching part of the job, even though I knew there would be pressure to win. More importantly, I wondered how my philosophy would go over during the interview. The hiring committee was a group of wonderful people who really made me feel at home. One member of that committee was a soon-to-be friend named Preston Headrick. Preston was one of the owners of the Greentop Barbecue, one of the best barbecue places in Alabama, and a major booster of Dora High School. He loved Dora with a passion and was always there for support when needed. When I accepted the job, it began a lifelong friendship that soon became an eternal one.

I guess Preston and the rest of the committee took a little flack when they hired me. Not long after getting the job, I was in the local sporting goods store when a stranger walked up to me and said with an analytical glance, "So you're the new coach? You're the guy that pulpit committee hired."

"Sir?"

"You know, that pulpit committee. You are a preacher, aren't you?"

"Well, I'm not really a preacher, but I do speak in churches." I was kind of shocked.

"Well, I thought we were after a coach." With that, he walked away. Thank goodness, we had a great season. I never saw that man again, but I knew right then that I was in the real world.

I saw Preston a lot at the field house and always after every game. He was a great supporter and one of those people you just couldn't help but like. He really had a gift with people. Everybody liked Preston Headrick. Through football, we became great friends, and I ate a lot of barbecue. I wish I could say that it was I who brought up Christ, but actually I think it was Preston. He was intrigued by the Christian philosophy of coaching I had, and he began to ask questions. Preston attended church, but he really hadn't committed His life to Christ. When he did make that decision, let me tell you that the passion he had for sports was exchanged for a passion that only Christ could have supplied. Preston not only accepted Christ as his savior, he asked Christ to enter his life, and things began to happen. All this did not happen overnight, but Preston began to grow in Christ. It seemed he could not get enough. His fire and enthusiasm for God were a blessing in my life. He had a sense of urgency to share Christ with others and to let Christ use his story to enter the lives of those around him. A few years later, Preston went into the ministry, Christ continuing to fill his life and overflowing into the world. He now pastors a church outside of Hamilton, Alabama. We don't see each other very much, mostly my fault. But I look forward to spending eternity with him. Most of all, I thank God for what He does when someone empties himself to be made full with the righteousness of Christ.

The beginning of the answer to the "call to live" begins at the feet of Jesus. It means we must replace ourselves with the presence of God through Christ.

Now we are ready for Christ to use our lives to change our world!

Building Bridges at Home

CHAPTER 5

Building Bridges at Home

The jailer called for lights, rushed in
and fell trembling before Paul and Silas.
He then brought them out and asked,
"Sirs, what must I do to be saved?"
They replied, "Believe in the Lord Jesus, and
you will be saved—you and your household."
Then they spoke the word of the Lord to him
and to all the others in his house. At that hour
of the night, the jailer took them and washed
their wounds; then immediately he and all his
family were baptized. The jailer brought them
into his house and set a meal before them, he
was filled with joy because he had come to
believe in God—he and his whole family.
—Acts 16: 29-34

Why is it that it is many times easier to tell a perfect stranger about Christ than it is to tell your own family? It's easier to meet someone on the street and witness to them than to your wife, easier to knock on the door of a stranger than to knock on door of your son's or daughter's room to share your faith. It's funny how the walls are thicker and taller in the relationships we have with our family; and most of the time, they are harder to tear down.

Let me say that I am not an educator who blames all the problems in our schools on the family. To be sure, there are plenty of problems we educators have caused and must solve in regard to our children. However, I do believe that the answer to some of the most severe problems we have in our society, as well as in education, have deep roots in the family. It seems that our homes have undergone some philosophical changes that have had some pretty profound results.

We need to remember that before there were other social institutions, there was the family. Before there were schools, before there were churches, before there was government, before we had an economy, well, in the beginning, there was family, and it was the only social institution. Its impact has been and, in spite of our advances, will always be a major factor in our own personal well-being and the stability of society as a whole.

One of the most important contributions that the family makes is that it sets the standards for the self-worth of individuals. Good, positive self-worth is absolutely essential if each of us is to reach his or her full potential and if we are going to thrive in our relationships. Over the past two generations, there have been quite a few changes regarding how we determine self-worth. Overall, the parents of the '30s, '40s, and '50s fostered a set of values and norms that in many ways are different from those of today. You and I recognize some of the phrases of that era…"take pride in your work," "an hour's work for an hour's pay," "your word is good enough," "say thank you and be appreciative for what you have," "do unto others as you would have them do unto you," "never kick a man when he is down," "respect your elders," "say please when you ask for something," and "it is better to give than to receive." Honor was what you did when nobody was looking, and character was sticking to your principles when everyone was looking. Time was something you spent with family and friends.

Now that's not to say that these parents did not make mistakes, and I'm not suggesting that the "good old days" were without their own set of problems. The Great Depression and several wars presented our society with tremendous challenges. Life was difficult, but through the difficulties, we grew as individuals and as a nation. It seemed that self-worth was based on strong inner qualities. Our grandparents and parents spent their whole lives giving to us, and their message to us was that it is the giving of ourselves to others that helps us find out who we are.

These generations have also been the backbone of the church. I have spoken in many churches through the years, and I see those dedicated saints, those men and women who have been there every time the doors of the church were open. They have been there in the good times and in the bad. They are tough, and they are dedicated to God and family. While my generation runs around from fad to fad, they are steady in their course.

Maybe it was their goodness to us that brought about the change. They were so intent on seeing that we had a better life than they did, not wanting us to have to work and suffer as much. Somehow, as life got easier and more convenient, something happened to self-worth. Those rock-solid inner qualities that made our country great gave way to a new set of standards that my generation seemed to embrace. A major change was about to occur. Self-worth began to be based on *the accumulation of wealth.* My generation became the "me" generation.

"Quality of work" was replaced with "profit margins." Handshakes were replaced with contracts. Bigger homes, newer cars, and larger salaries became the goals of the new generation. Phrases like "you owe it to yourself" or "you deserve a break today" only reinforced the worship of self. We began to wear our labels on the outside of our clothes so everyone could see our expensive brand names. Why not? Wearing expensive clothes meant you were a better person. Right? The more expensive gift you gave someone, the more you loved them—a truth from the new vision of self-worth.

I remember when I was five that a shiny new fire truck is what every little boy wanted. Why? Because firemen and policemen had "neat" jobs. Self-worth was based on giving to others, and those occupations represented public servants who helped us in times of need. One little boy would go up to another on the playground and say, "What does your daddy do?"

"My daddy's a fireman" would be the answer.

"Wow! That's neat. I wish my dad was a fireman."

What happens to that conversation when self-worth is based on the accumulation of wealth? The statement would be, "My dad's better that your dad because my dad makes more money." Even worse is, "I am better than you because I've got more stuff." The status of the parent is directly related to how much material gain the family has. Children go home and say, "Why can't I have so-and-so like Tommy?" Too often, this seems to be the language of the playgrounds of the "me" generation.

On September 11, 2001, America quickly returned to our roots. One of the results of that day was a powerful appreciation for what firemen and policemen do in this country, how they risk their lives for us each day. At West Point, we had three students dressed as firemen strike that famous pose with the American flag before a Friday night football game. All of a sudden, it was "cool" to be a fireman regardless of how underpaid they seemed to be.

There are a couple of problems with basing self-worth on the accumulation of wealth. To be sure, we have a lot of stuff. Our houses are nicer, and there are some great video games out. But what happens to those inner qualities when our self-worth is based on materialism? What happens to respect for others when your image of yourself is based on a car or clothes? What happens to taking pride in your work when you are given everything without having to work for it? *Honor* and *character* become military terms when outside items replace inner qualities. And what about morals and ethics? When relationships are replaced by the worship of self, isn't it inevitable that morals come crashing down? Phrases like "it's my life, and I'll do what I want" and "mind your own business" are replies made by those who define who they are by how much they can get.

Let me be clear that I love the young people of today, and in no way do I blame them for the dilemmas we face. On the contrary, I think we have the greatest generation of young people we have ever had in this country. It is our generation that has created this monster; I pray we don't leave this mess solely to our children to sort out. What kind of message do we send to our kids when we go on television and declare a "war on drugs!" right before we go to our cocktail parties or light up our cigarettes?

The real problem with basing self-worth on the accumulation of wealth is that is a lie—a very big lie. The assumption is that if you get enough stuff, then you will be happy and have inner peace with who you are. All around us, we see evidence to the contrary. Our children grow up only to find that the very thing they have been taught as the very foundation of life is instead "sinking sand," that material things do not make you happy, and that building your life around yourself only leads to frustration and hopelessness.

We need to take a strong look at our families not for the sake of education but for the sake of our children and spouses. Our call to live for Christ starts at home.

I was driving down the road one day, listening to James Dobson, for whom I have great respect. Dr. Dobson has touched the lives of many Americans and has spent his life showing us how to make a difference in our families. Dr. Dobson said that with the many lives that his ministry has had the opportunity to touch—the many articles he has written, the many lectures he has given, the Focus on the Family seminars—with all this, that he would be a failure if his own children didn't accept Christ as their Savior.

What a powerful statement that is to each of us as Christian parents!

Family is a central theme in the Bible. The importance of Mary and Joseph are portrayed in the life of Jesus. We all know the story of John the Baptist's parents, Zechariah and Elizabeth. One of the most powerful stories of the Old Testament is the one about Abraham and Isaac. Abraham's test of faith was to be willing to sacrifice his own son out of his obedience to God. Our own salvation is the willingness of God to sacrifice His own Son for our sins. God didn't send just anyone to die for us. He sent the best He had—His only Son. Certainly, this should tell us exactly how important family is in God's plan.

The New Testament is full of stories about family. In the fifth chapter of Mark, we read about a father named Jarius who had a sick daughter. He goes to Jesus to ask Him to come heal her. On His way, Jesus heals another woman of a long illness and arrives at the little girl's house too late, or so it seems. Jesus says that the girl is only sleeping and heals her. I think about what would have happened to the daughter and to the woman with cancer if Jarius had not been the father that he was.

The Syrophoenician woman begs Jesus to cast the demons out of her daughter. She was a Greek, and Jesus's response to her was, "First let the children eat all they want, for it is not right to take the children's bread and toss it to the dogs."

Her response to Christ was a powerful one, full of a mother's love for her child. "Yes, Lord, but even the dogs under the table eat the children's crumbs."

Jesus recognizes her love and her faith and heals the daughter.

A father approaches Jesus in the ninth chapter of Mark. This time, he actually brings his son who is possessed by a demon and places him at Jesus's feet. When asked if he believes, the father replies, "I do believe. Help me overcome my unbelief!" Jesus heals the son, helps him to his feet, and gets him something to eat—all the results of a parent bringing a child to Christ.

The scripture quoted at the beginning of this chapter is from the book of Acts. Paul and Silas are in prison when an earthquake hits, and the prison doors are opened. The jailer wakes up and realizes that the prisoners have escaped. Knowing the consequences he will face, he is about to take his own life when Paul calls out to him, "Don't harm yourself. We are still here." Can you imagine the shock on the jailer's face when he realizes that Paul and Silas have not escaped? Instead, they have saved his life by their actions, which results in the salvation of the jailer and all his family. Several times, his family is mentioned in this scripture. The same phrase is used about Cornelius when he invites Peter to his house to preach. Cornelius has his whole family in attendance, and all accept Christ and are baptized.

It is obvious that both Cornelius and the jailer had strong relationships with their families. Once each of them experienced and accepted Christ, the bridges were already built for Jesus to walk across into the lives of family members. It was through the relationships with these two men that wives and children were able to find Christ. What a wonderful opportunity each of us has to be used by

God to reach others in our families. We are called each day to build bridges, and it is as important a calling as we will ever have.

Every day I walk into West Point High School and try to be the principal of about 550 teenagers. Maybe God can use me to make a difference in the lives of one of those young people. Sometimes we never know. But one thing I do know: I know I can make a difference in the lives of two young people, Wesley and Ryan Coleman.

Let me take a minute to mention my family. I've already mentioned my parents; my wife, Shireen; and our two sons, Wesley and Ryan. I really don't know how anyone could be blessed any more than through those relationships. I have not mentioned Shireen's parents, Tom and Marie, and her sister Stacy, all of whom I love very much. You see, we don't have in-laws or outlaws; we only have family. We spend all our Christmases and Thanksgivings together. We go to college football games together. We spend spring break, the Fourth of July, and Labor Days together. I know that we are unique in this respect, but we wouldn't have it any other way. There were nine of us until a couple of years ago when my father went to be with God. Now there are eight and one in spirit. When Wesley and Ryan get married, our circle will grow, but I think we will continue to do things together.

When I think of how blessed our family is, I have some difficulty relating to the many problems encountered by young people to whom I have talked. I have to remember how fortunate I have been and try to understand how hard it is on kids who have not had the support that I have had. My heart goes out to them, and I try to emphasize that while things are not what they need to be right now, one day, they can build a family of support. One day, they will be the parents, making the decisions that lay the foundation for their family. One day, God will be using them to build a family on the Solid Rock.

I also had wonderful relationships with my grandparents, all of whom now live in heaven. No matter how many games you lose or what the score is, your grandmother always has a cookie, and your grandfather always wants to cut a watermelon. They want you to be successful, but mostly they just love you, unconditionally. God has used them and our parents to pass the torch to us. It's our turn to carry on.

I was especially close to my mother's parents, Meme and Daddy Pop. Daddy Pop loved to fish as much as anyone I have ever known. Now we had a relative, Aunt Grace, who lived on a farm outside Atlanta, and on that farm was one of the finest bass ponds in the country. Each year, Daddy Pop would plan the fishing trip, with visions of wall hanging bass in his mind. When I became sixteen, I became the official driver for the trip. I would drive Meme and Daddy Pop over to Aunt Grace's, and we would have a great three or four days. Daddy Pop and I would fish out of an old wooden boat. Daddy Pop had all the latest fads in the fishing industry, though it seemed to me that Meme caught most of the fish with a cane pole and a jar of worms.

One day on one of our visits, Daddy Pop noticed a huge wasp nest in the corner of the boathouse. He immediately came up with the master plan. I would sit far up on the bank and watch while he took care of the problem. He took a long cane fishing pole and stuck a wad of newspapers on the end. Wearing a large plastic raincoat, he carefully floated the boat out into the water, close enough to the wasps that he could reach the nest with the pole. I smiled as I watched my ninety-two-year-old grandfather prepare to do battle. It did look a bit odd. Finally, Daddy Pop took a match and lit the newspapers. He slowly approached the nest with the ball of fire. One small problem: as he focused on the nest, the paper began to touch the water, and soon I noticed a large circle of steam begin to rise from the lake. Before I could say anything, a very surprised Daddy Pop stuck a bunch of wet newspapers up to a very large wasp nest. The wasps were not too happy, and as they swarmed, Daddy Pop had to lie down in the bottom of the boat, covered by the raincoat. At first I was afraid he might get stung, but when I saw he was safe, I began to laugh. I laughed, and I laughed. I rolled on the bank for a good ten minutes before I could go down and hear Daddy Pop's account of what happened. Great ones are the only memories I have of my grandparents.

My extended family of aunts, uncles, and cousins have always been very special, and while I haven't spent as much time with them as I would have liked, I know that they are there. Those "family reunions" I used to dread as a teenager are now sacred experiences that bring much joy and a strong feeling of security.

Needless to say, I thank God for my family, the blessings of the past and the blessings that are to come.

One of the biggest mistakes we have made in this country is when we began to substitute *things for our children for time spent with our children.* Over the past twenty years, day-care centers have become one of the fastest growing businesses in our nation. I realize that many times they are very positive alternatives in the lives of families. Sometimes they are necessary. But I also think they are symptoms of a society that equates self-worth with the accumulation of wealth. As we think we need more, we work more. The more we work, the more we can provide things for our families. Unfortunately, this comes with quite a price tag. The cost of this mentality is less time with our children. There is no substitute for time in any relationship.

I have spent almost twenty-five years in education. I see teenagers with nice cars and plenty of spending money. They have computer programs and video games with which they spend hours of their time. They have nice clothes to wear and plenty of places to go. But they are starving for one thing: time spent with their parents. I have known these youth as their coach, their teacher, and as their principal, but neither I nor anyone else in education have ever been able to take the place of their mother or their father. Those are unique relationships that cannot be replaced by anyone else, and they certainly will not be replaced by "things" of wealth. While the toys get more expensive, the distance between parent and child gets further apart.

I remember a time in my life when I was consumed with coaching and winning football games. My oldest son, Wesley, was just getting old enough to enjoy playing sports, so naturally I bought him all the right things: an adjustable goal he could shoot basketball on, even dunk if he wanted to; an insidious device called a "throwback machine" that could play catch with a child with no one else around; a tee that would hold a football for the player to kick. Oh, yes, we had all the latest in sporting equipment. I would come home and give Wesley pep talks on using these new devices and question why he wasn't spending more time practicing. Thank God, I finally realized that Wesley didn't want portable goals, throwback machines, and do-it-yourself football tees. What Wesley wanted and, more important, what he needed was a father who would shoot baskets with him, play catch with him, and hold the football while he kicked it. He wanted to trade all the "stuff" in for a father who would spend time with him.

There is a song that I have quoted many times when speaking to groups, especially when the audience is composed of men. It was made famous in the late sixties by Harry Chapin. I'm sure you've heard of it, and I might not have the words just right, but it goes something like this:

> My son arrived just the other day.
> He came to the world in the usual way.
> But there were planes to catch and bills to pay.
> He learned to walk while I was away.
> And he was talking before I knew it and as he
>   grew,
> He said, "I'm gonna be like you dad, you know
>   I'm gonna be like you."
>
> And the cat's in the cradle with a silver spoon,
> Little boy blues, man in the moon.
> "When you coming home, Dad?"
> "I don't know when, we'll get together then son.
> You know we'll have a good time then."
>
> My son turned ten just the other day.
> He said thanks for the ball bat, come on let's play
> Can you teach me to throw? I said, "Not today.
> I got a lot to do." He said, "that's OK"
> And as he walked away he smiled and said, "I'm
>   gonna be like him, you know I'm gonna "be
>   like him."

The song goes on, but reality hits on the last verse.

> He's older now, my son moved away
> I called him up just the other day.
> I said, "I like to see you if you don't mind."
> He said, "I'd love to Dad, if I could find the time.
> You see the new job's a hassle and the kid's with
> the flu,
> But it was sure nice talking to you Dad, it was
> sure nice talking to you"
> And as I hung up the phone, it occurred to me,
> My son was just like me, my boy was just like me.
>
> And the cat's in the cradle with a silver spoon
> Little boy blue, man in the moon.
> "When you coming home son?" "I don't know
> when
> We'll get together then Dad,
> You know we'll have a good time, then."

It is a great song with a powerful truth. If we raise our children believing that materialism is the key to life, then what will happen to us one day when we need their relationships? Will they substitute "things" for time spent with parents? It is one of Satan's biggest lies.

I use the words to that song when we study the family in our sociology class. We spend almost six weeks on every possible aspect of family life. Students are to look at their lives as future parents. Through the years, these students have expressed how they long to share time and experiences with their families. Their testimonies bear out the truth that we have made a great mistake in this country thinking that "stuff" replaces time. We talk about "if you tell your child every day that you love them, then they will never feel 'weird' when you say it." That "if you talk to your child every day, then they will never feel awkward when you talk to them." Many students vow they will uphold these promises of parenting. They insist they will not make the same mistakes my generation has made. I believe them.

We are in a great war for our children. We know that God has a great plan, but we must remember that Satan also has a plan, a plan that brings the fight to our turf. Maybe a major part of it is to get us so preoccupied with the problems and opportunities of the world that we leave our homes unguarded. While we're doing battle in the world, Satan wants to come through the back door and take our families hostage. He knows that if he can take our children and spouses, he can destroy our ministries in the world.

During my coaching days at Benjamin Russell High School, I became acquainted with a retired Air Force officer who was living on Martin Lake outside of Alexander City, Alabama. Even though I only knew him a few short years, Ernie became one of my closest friends. He and his wife, Harriet, became members of the church where I was pastor. Our families had some great times at their house on the lake. I showed him some tricks about crappie fishing, and being retired, he proceeded to try to catch every crappie Martin Lake had to offer.

A few months after meeting Ernie, I found out that he was diagnosed with cancer. He never complained, but as time went on, the disease began to take its toll. Those last few days, I spent a lot of time in his hospital room. We talked about successful fishing trips, but as time drew closer, Ernie began to talk about more serious things. He had a wonderful relationship with God and with Harriet. He did, however, have some concerns about what he perceived to be his failures as a father. He expressed to me how he had been so dedicated to his job that he had neglected his children. He had always been one who was in control, but the last few years, he had realized that he wasn't in control. God was. While those relationships had greatly improved, he wished he had made important decisions earlier in his life when his children were younger. He told me things to tell his son after his passing, things that he wished he could have said himself. I promised him that I would share his story about how important family is. He was a fine Christian and did more for others in his last few years than many of us will do in a lifetime. I praise God that Ernie now enjoys a concept of family he never thought possible.

Remember the Hindu girl, how she said, "Jesus built a bridge from her heart to mine and just walked over." Some of the most important bridges Christ will ever build will be the ones in our families. Why? Because more than anyone else, we have the greatest chance to make a difference in those lives. Sometimes we read the scripture where Jesus says if we love our families more than Him, we are not worthy of the kingdom of heaven, and we think that somehow cheapens our love for family. On the contrary, with Christ in our lives, we can love our family far more than we ever could without Him. Jesus Christ is the basis for our self-worth: not things, not jobs, and not money. We are called to build those bridges, to bring our families to Christ, just as the jailer did, just as Cornelius did. For many of us, it is our greatest area of ministry.

The Passing of the Story

As I sat in the shooting house, I did what I always do when I go hunting on the family farm. I thought about my dad. We were about as close as father and son could be. He never missed one of my ball games, either as a player or as a coach. He and my mom were always there.

One of the greatest parts of our relationship was our great love for the outdoors. My dad always had time to take me fishing and hunting. I guess quail hunting was our passion. My dad always had bird dogs, and I have kept the tradition going even though my sons seem to enjoy deer hunting more. Quail hunting in Alabama is not what it used to be, but deer hunting is great. If you judge success on killing a deer, then Wesley, Ryan, and I are not very adept. But if you judge it on fun and quality time together, and I do, then our deer hunting is a huge success. Our rules were and still are if you don't eat it, you don't hunt it. To this day, quail with biscuits, mashed potatoes, and gravy is still my favorite meal. Deer meat is probably a distant third behind crappie fillets.

Most of the time, my father and I hunted together when I was growing up and on into adulthood. On occasions when he couldn't get off work, I would go with some of our other hunting buddies. I was always practicing some sport, so sometimes Dad would go with some of the same friends. Regardless of who went hunting when, you can be sure one of us would call the other to get the details of the hunt.

"How did you do today?" one would ask the other. Then a step-by-step analysis began with great attention to every covey that was found, every point a dog made, and every shot that was fired. Slowly, the hunt was shared until we embraced the same memory. It was if we had hunted together.

As I sat in the deer stand, I realized how much I missed those phone calls. My dad was pretty sick when we built the shooting house I was in that day. I remembered how we sat him in a chair so he could watch us build it. He would doze off to sleep from time to time, but I knew there was no place he would rather be. He loved the old farm, and he loved being with us regardless of how he felt. I thought how great it would be to go home that day, hear the phone ring, and be able to share the hunt with him. I wondered if he perhaps was watching from heaven, but I guess heaven has too many other great things going on to worry with hunting.

When I got home that night, I admit I was pretty heavyhearted. The silence of the hunt had given way to a lot of sad memories.

The hope came that night when the phone rang.

"Hello?"

"Dad, this is Wesley. Did you go to the farm today?"

"Yes, I went."

"Well, how did it go? Tell me about it."

"Fine," I said as tears began to fill my eyes. And then I began to share the hunt with my son. Every moment, every detail was shared until the hunt became a shared experience. A great awareness fell over me that the telling of the story had been passed, that I had taken my father's place, and that Wesley and Ryan had taken mine. God spoke to me that night, and I'm not sure I've been the same since. Each day I take on more of my dad's role. I can only pray that each day I can take more of Christ's role for me.

You and I are called to carry on. It's our turn to pass the story on. It's our turn to share the truth.

Building Bridges with Others

CHAPTER 6

Building Bridges with Others

> Suppose one of you has a hundred sheep and
> loses one of them. Does he not leave the ninety-
> nine in the open country and go after the lost
> sheep until he finds it? And when he finds it,
> he joyfully puts it on his shoulders and goes
> home. Then he calls his friends and neighbors
> together and says, 'Rejoice with me; I have
> found my lost sheep.' I tell you that in the same
> way there will be more rejoicing in heaven over
> one sinner who repents than over ninety-nine
> righteous persons who do not need to repent.
> —Luke 15: 3–7

We live in a society that gets very caught up in numbers. We keep up with how many were in attendance at the game, how many home runs someone hits, how many points are scored, how many went to see the opening of a movie, how many records were sold, and how many watched the final 4 championship game. Of course, when you live in a society that places such a high priority on wealth and prestige, then it's easy to understand. These numbers mean money and personal accomplishment. More is better in terms of finance and self-worth.

On the other hand, we need to be careful that we don't let this worldly mentality bleed over into our Christian faith. As I have mentioned, I was the pastor of a wonderful church while I was in college. Our district, made up of sixty-seven churches, had a contest to see how much growth we could have in one year. A 10 percent increase in attendance would earn you a gold star, a percentage of profession of faiths got another star, and so on. Four gold stars represented the most you could earn, and at the end of the year, churches would be recognized at our annual district meeting. Now this was right down my alley! My athletic side took over, and we immediately began working to reach our goals. One by one, each of our stars were earned, and you know what? At the district meeting, with all the large churches in our district, our little church was the only one that received four gold stars. That's right! We got a nice certificate, which we promptly framed and put on the wall in the fellowship hall. I'm surprised I didn't put it right under the lighted cross in the front of the sanctuary. I've matured a lot in the faith since those days. I was sincere, even though my motives were a little off.

While numbers are nice, we must remember that numbers represent individual people. God sees each of us individually, not as a number in the human race. What changed your life is not that Jesus died for the world. What changed your life is that *Jesus died for you.* What changed my life is that *Jesus died for me.* Jesus died for each of us individually. He knows us, and with all the people that are in the world, he wants to have an individual relationship with each one of us!

Jesus tells a story in the fifteenth chapter of Luke that goes against the views of the world. He tells of a shepherd who has one hundred sheep and loses one. "Does he not leave the ninety-nine in the open country and go after the lost sheep until he finds it?"

And what would be our answer? "Well, maybe that's what you would do two thousand years ago, but not in America in the twenty-first century. Are you kidding me? It's only one sheep, easily replaceable. Sometimes, you've got to cut your losses. You know, play the odds. What happens if while you are gone, something happens to the others? Now there's the real tragedy. And after all, you're probably not going to find it anyway."

Jesus isn't finished. He goes on to say that when the shepherd finally finds the lost sheep, he calls his friends and neighbors together to rejoice about the recovery. Finally, he concludes with a powerful statement. "I tell you that in the same way, there will be more rejoicing in heaven over one sinner who repents than over ninety-nine righteous persons who do not need to repent."

Think about an event you have been to when the crowd was wild and there was electricity in the air. I have coached in a few high school football games when I could not even hear myself talk. The excitement was unbelievable. I've attended some college games when the crowd was worked into a frenzy. And while I've never been to a Super Bowl game, I can imagine the excitement that surrounds the biggest football game of the year.

Picture in your mind that you're standing at the free throw line in the national championship game. Fifty thousand fans are screaming their heads off. A national television audience is sitting on the edge of their recliners. An entire nation is holding its breath. You pause for a moment to take it all in. Then you focus on the goal, and with ice water in your veins, you calmly knock down the winning shot. The crowd erupts into hysteria. You get the picture?

Now get this. The situation I have just described is only a drop in the bucket when compared to how all of heaven reacted when you repented of your sins and accepted Christ as your savior. Hey, I'm talking about you and me, not some famous actor or athlete, not some historical figure. Heaven went crazy over you! The heavenly hosts looked down at Satan and said, "Look on the scoreboard and see whose behind—you, you, you, you!" Now that's eternal excitement!

Jesus goes on in the same chapter and tells of a woman who has ten coins and loses one. When she finds the coin, everyone celebrates with her. He concludes, "There is rejoicing in the presence of the angels of God when one sinner repents."

The final story in the "lost" chapter is about a lost son. When the prodigal finally returns from his sinful journey, his father rejoices and throws a party. "But we had to celebrate and be glad," he tells the confused brother, "because this brother of yours was dead and is alive again. He was lost and is found."

It is very important that we see and understand this truth, that we don't let the world distract us with the numbers game. We are to extend Christ to the world, one person at a time. If the world is to be saved, it will be saved one person at a time.

When we look at Jesus's ministry, we clearly see that he was concerned with individual relationships. Yes, he was a great teacher and preacher, sometimes speaking to thousands of people at a time, and without a microphone at that! But when you look closer, he always had time for individuals. He called his disciples one at a time. He sought out the sick woman who touched his garment, he called out to the tax collector in the sycamore tree, he knelt down to forgive the adulteress, he met with Nicodemus in the darkness, and he forgave the thief on the cross. He offers each of us an individual relationship with Him, and He calls us to extend that relationship with others. He wants to build bridges with friends, neighbors, and strangers.

In the second chapter of Mark, Jesus is speaking in a house so full of people that not one more person could get in, not even outside the door. Oh, that our churches would be so crowded. A paralytic is brought to the house by four of his friends. Seeing no way to get in, the four friends take him up to the roof and lower him down in front of Jesus on a stretcher. Can you picture it? While Jesus is preaching, probably right in the middle of His third main point, the roof begins to fall in. Now this is no ordinary hole being made. This is a hole large enough to lower a man down on a bed of some sort. Needless to say, very large clods of dirt began falling down in the room that Jesus is in. Out of the corner of his eye, Peter probably tries to sneak a look into the face of the owner of the house. Everyone looks up after the man is lowered, only to see the sheepish faces of four men in the hole above. One is shrugging his shoulder as if to say, "It's the only thing we could think of." Jesus stops in the middle of His talk and does what Jesus always did. He dealt with the needs of the one. Not only does He forgive the man of his sins, He also commands him to "take up your bed and walk," which the man immediately does.

But what of the four friends? They obviously believed in Jesus and would have loved to have been in the house, listening to what the master said. They weren't sure exactly how, but they knew if they brought their paralyzed friend into His presence, Christ would do the rest. Because of their friendship to the man, "all of heaven" rejoiced on that day. One who was lost had been found.

We are also to be reminded that in the case of individual relationships, we all have a ministry. We may never speak to a group or ever teach a Sunday school class. We may never lead a church service or sing a special on Sunday morning. But what each of us can do is build a bridge through a friendship, to make a difference in the life of one person. This ministry of reaching out to individuals is the most powerful one in the church today. And we are all called to be a part of that ministry.

Harold was the best crappie fisherman I have ever known. He taught me everything I know about catching the best-tasting fish God ever created. The first time he asked me to go fishing with him, I thought I was being given an award. It was an honor. Within two short hours, we had the limit: well, maybe a little over the limit. We had a great time, and soon there was another trip and more fish. But something else besides fishing started happening in that boat. Harold and I were in the early stages of a great friendship that continued to grow like the numbers of fish we were catching.

Harold was a great guy but had never been to church. One Sunday, I was surprised and glad to see Harold and his wife, Nancy, sitting close to the back of the church. At the end of the service, it was my custom to pray at the altar during the invitation. I couldn't help but hear the sound of the door closing as if someone was leaving. A few moments later, I heard the door again, and as I ended my prayer and looked up, there was Harold and Nancy at the altar. They had left the church for a moment, but in the parking lot, they decided to return. They came down to the altar and committed their lives to Christ. Harold took his commitment like he did his fishing—very seriously and faithful to Christ ever since that day. Nancy has been a wonderful Sunday school teacher for many years.

On Saturdays, a lot of the men in the community would meet during deer season at the church and go hunting together. The fellowship was great, and bridges were built. Several men and their families began attending church and made commitments to Christ.

I was sharing with an older minister the concept of how fishing and hunting could be used by God to reach others. He strongly disagreed and suggested this kind of wishful thinking wasn't in the plan. "Billy, can you name me one person who accepted Christ in a fishing boat?"

Not wanting to be disrespectful, I politely said, "What about Peter and Andrew?" I don't think he liked the reply.

Too often, we think of witnessing as a defining moment in time, limited by minutes on a clock with specific words we carefully map out. Sometimes, witnessing is simply a friendship, and the message is sent over time through our actions and the experiences we share with one another.

When we hang around our friends, we began to take on some of their habits and ways. Ever had someone come up to you and say, "You've been hanging around John so long that you're becoming just like him." Most of the time, these statements have negative connotations like we're picking up some bad habits. But can't we pick up good things too? It stands to reason that if you hang around Christians long enough, you might become like them. You might want to accept Christ for yourself.

To be sure, we are called to confess Christ with our lips. But more importantly, we are to live for Christ, and through our actions, we are his witnesses to others.

We also need to remember that it is not the quantity of time we spend with others. It is the quality of that time that helps the relationship grow.

The Emmaus Walk is a three-day course on Christianity where a group of men and women learn and share about the truth of Christ for the better part of seventy-two hours. It is amazing to me how a group of strangers can in three short days become lifelong friends, but that is exactly what happens. It is a reminder of how I have allowed distractions to interfere with the quality of the relationships I have in my life. I have been blessed immeasurably through the friendships I have developed through the Emmaus community and thank God for what happens when Christ is in the center of any relationship.

Jesus reminds us in the scripture of the importance of the one. Could it be possible that there is someone in the world that only you could reach for Christ, only you who has the opportunity to build the bridge for Christ to walk over? I think about all the players I've had the pleasure of coaching, all the students I've taught, all the opportunities, some of which I've taken advantage of, many of which I have not.

I think about the kid who sits alone in the lunchroom every day or the one who can't dress as nicely as everyone else. I think about the cantankerous old man who is dying of loneliness and who so desperately needs a friend. I think of the one who out of desperation tries too hard to be a friend and the one who lashes out because of undeserved circumstances in his life. I think of those Jesus referred to as "the least of these." I think of those who have nothing but their wealth, who unsuccessfully try to buy their friendships. There are so many needs, so many opportunities for ministry.

Most of us don't even know the names of the neighbor three houses down the block. We don't have relationships with a majority of the members of our church. We don't know the interests of the people we work with or their needs. We need to look around us, forget about tomorrow, and focus on the opportunities of this day.

John 1:42 says, "And Andrew brought Peter to Jesus." Peter was the rock, the guy who got the keys to the kingdom, the disciple who preached at Pentecost. Yet it was Andrew who brought Peter to Jesus.

We must remember that we don't have to solve the problems of our friends and neighbors. We don't have to have the answers to all their questions. Like Andrew, if we can just bring them to Jesus, He'll take care of the rest. All we have to do is let Jesus build the bridge, to seek out and develop the relationship. God will take it from there.

Probably no one in the world has reached more people for Christ than Billy Graham. Dr. Graham has dedicated his life to reaching lost souls, and God has greatly blessed his ministry. But you know what? Someone brought Billy Graham to Christ.

I once heard a story about a small revival that took place several years ago. Throughout the week, no one had made a decision for Christ, until finally on Friday, a young man came down and dedicated his life to God. That young man was Billy Graham. Do you think "all of heaven" rejoiced when that lost sheep was brought home? Think about the millions of lives that have been touched because of what happened on that Friday night.

I've thought a lot about that story. Every day I have the opportunity to allow God to use me to touch a life. Maybe my whole purpose is to lead the next Billy Graham to Christ. He might be going to West Point High School. Or maybe it's just to reach out to anyone, for to God his or her soul is just as important.

Everybody needs a friend. Friendship is a very powerful channel God can use to flow into the life of another person. Even strangers are watching our lives, and we never know when an opportunity to witness through our actions will present itself.

At my first coaching job at Benjamin Russell, we started a tradition of players and coaches gathering at the middle of the field for prayer after the football game. While that seems to be fairly common today, it had not yet caught on in the late 1970s. I remember the last game of the year was at Phoenix City, and we got blown away. I was the defensive coordinator, and Phoenix City scored just about every time they had the ball. Embarrassed and humiliated, I stumbled out to the center of the field for prayer. I honestly don't remember saying any of the words to the Lord's Prayer. I was too busy thinking how bad I wanted to get out of there. When we finished, we slowly began to walk off the field in front of the home crowd. To my amazement, they began to give us a standing ovation in support of the prayer we, or at least I, thoughtlessly said. Even in our failures, God uses our actions to reach out to others, sometimes more powerfully in our failures.

For twenty-five years, I have used a story that exemplifies the philosophy of serving Christ I want to have. I have told this story so many times that people have called me to ask if they could use it, thinking it was my story. I've told it in churches. I've told it in class and at graduations. It is not my story, and I'm not really sure where or when I first heard it. You've probably heard it or seen it in one form or another. All I know is that it has changed my life.

A little boy was walking down the beach one day and noticed that millions of starfish had washed up on the shore. Having compassion for the starfish, the boy began picking them up and throwing them in the ocean.

An old man noticed the boy, walked up to him, and said, "What are you doing, son?"

"I'm just picking up starfish and throwing them in the ocean."

The old man stopped the boy. He pointed down the beach and said, "The beach is long, and there are millions of starfish. You can't make a difference."

Undaunted, the boy picked up a starfish and threw it in the ocean.

This action sort of aggravated the old man. The boy obviously was not listening. The old man grabbed him by the shirt, pointed out to the ocean, and said, "The ocean is deep and vast, and there are millions of starfish. You can't make a difference."

The boy picked up a starfish, threw it in the ocean, and said, "*It made a difference to that one.*"

It made a difference to that one!

When West Point High School burned to the ground in 1996, we were faced with one of the biggest challenges I have ever been associated with. I remember walking into my new office, a six-by-eight room at the end of a trailer, and wondering if we were going to be able to pull it off. We were working eighteen hours a day, and everyone was pretty much exhausted physically and emotionally. Our goal was to have the students back in school in four days. I dragged into the room and plopped down in a donated chair, pretty much whipped and for the first time starting to ask the question, "Why?" I looked over to my left, and there on a built-in counter at the end of the trailer lay a poster with the starfish story written on it. There was a beach and a little boy throwing starfish into the ocean. In that moment, God reminded me that He was still in control and that there were more important things than replacing a school. There were kids coming back in a couple of days—opportunities to "make a difference to that one."

I asked everyone I could think of who left the poster in my office. No one claimed responsibility. I only know that God used that moment to reaffirm what we are all called to do in Christ.

When Christ died on the cross, he had you and me in mind. You and I were the ones He made a difference to. You were "that one." I was "that one." He now calls us to make a difference to "that one," and in doing so, He uses us to change the world.

Another story says that Jesus went up to heaven, and the angels asked, "Master, what's the great plan?"

Jesus said, "I made a difference to that one, and that one made a difference to that one, and that one made a difference to that one."

A little confused, the angels replied, "But what if that plan doesn't work?" to which Jesus replied, "There is no other plan."

Through individual relationships, we all have a ministry. Each of us is called to make a difference for Christ, one person at a time. Our witness is a "call to live," to allow Jesus to use our life to build a bridge and just walk over into the life of another.

Who's to Blame?

CHAPTER 7

---◦◦◦◦◦---

Who's to Blame?

> As he went along, he saw a man blind
> from birth. His disciples asked him,
> "Rabbi, who sinned, this man or his
> parents, that he was born blind?"
> "Neither this man nor his parents sinned,"
> said Jesus, "but this happened so that the
> work of God might be displayed in his life."
> —John 9:1–3

It seemed like the logical question. After all, the man *was* blind. There had to be sin somewhere. The prevalent feeling was that blindness, along with leprosy and paralysis, was the result of sin. On the other hand, this man was born blind. Perhaps it was the sins of his parents. Exodus 4:6 says, "For I, the Lord your God, am a jealous God, punishing the children for the sin of the fathers to the third and fourth generation of those who hate me." Anyway, whether it was the man or his parents, someone had to be blamed.

Sometimes we forget that Jesus's disciples were devout Jews who firmly believed that salvation was based on adherence to the law. And the law always gives you someone to blame—someone breaks the rules, someone does not measure up, someone makes a mistake. Furthermore, it was concluded that those who suffered with various difficulties had brought these situations upon themselves through their failures to keep the law.

Such was the case with the man born blind. The disciples simply asked what everyone else had been thinking for years. "Rabbi, who is to blame that this man was born blind? Was it his sins or the sins of his parents?"

The answer that Jesus gave through His words and through His actions was quite remarkable. To really answer "the call to live," we need to carefully consider how Jesus's response applies to our everyday life.

There's a lot of blaming going on in our world today. Whose fault is it that we have higher gasoline prices? Is it the Middle Eastern countries, American oil companies, or our own dependence on the car? Why do our morals seem to be on the slide? Is it the media's fault? Is Hollywood to blame? Or is it our inability to say no? How about divorce? The husband says it's the wife's fault. The wife says it's the husband's fault. Of course, all the problems of today are blamed on the younger generation. They are going to the dogs, you know. Who's to blame for higher taxes? Our two parties are quick to point the finger at the other as the source of all our problems. How about terrorism? Who's to blame for global warming or unemployment or teenage pregnancy? Whose fault is it things are not like they were in "the good old days"?

Even in the church, we play the "blaming game." One side of the church blames the other side, and vice versa. And of course, everyone knows it's the preacher's fault if things are not going like they should. His sermons are too long or too short or "over my head" or too simple or not biblical, or don't relate to today. He does not visit enough, or he is never in the office. Or as the song goes, "He didn't even shake my hand!"

By now you get the picture. We are not so different from the disciples. For every problem in the world, the first order of business is to find out whose fault it is. From the White House to the teacher's lounge to our breakfast table, we play the game, and we play it well.

We can group all our blaming into three distinct categories. The first are those who blame everything in life that is bad on someone else. It's always someone else's fault.

Take football, for example. I send in a running play, and it fails miserably. I take out the back and say, "What happened out there?" The back says, "There wasn't a hole, coach. There was no blocking."

I pull out the tackle and say, "What happened?" The tackle replies, "The back must have hit the wrong hole. I had my man blocked." This process continues until we have the chance to look at the film, which by the way is after the game is over, and it's too late to make a difference.

In the meantime, fans are quick to remind us that it's the coach's fault for calling such terrible plays. "Coach runs when we ought to pass. He passes when we ought to run. Coach plays the wrong boys, especially when it's my son on the bench." Of course, one problem is that we assess the coach's play-calling ability *after* the play is over, and we determine who should be playing without attending practices.

But in the end, we can always play our trump card, the one we've been saving in case all else fails. Everyone knows that really it's the referee's fault when the team is losing. "We would have won if the official hadn't blown that call at the end of the game. I don't know what it is, but those officials always seem to be out to get us. Where did those guys come from anyway?"

In the fall of 1994, West Point High School had the only undefeated team in school history. It was a wonderful season, primarily because we had a lot of good players, and we were also very fortunate with injuries. But there is one thing we did that I really think made a difference. We adopted the motto "No excuses, no regrets." It became our theme for the year. Before the season, we dedicated ourselves to making no excuses for our failures. No one would blame anyone else or anything else. From the coaches to the players to the managers, each of us would take responsibility for our actions; excuses would not be acceptable. I don't know if it helped us win any games, but it sure "felt" good. Even when we lost our third-round playoff game, we lost with no excuses—we knew that we had done our best.

In the fifth chapter of John, we find the story of the man who was healed at the pool of Bethesda. Jesus seemingly asked him a very unusual question. Seeing that he had been lying there for a long time, Jesus asked, "Do you want to be healed?"

Listen to the man's response. "Sir, I have no one to help me into the pool when the water is stirred. While I am trying to get in, someone else goes down ahead of me." In other words, the man was saying to Jesus, "Sir, you have misperceived the problem. You see, it not my fault." Then he proceeds to tell Jesus whose fault it is that he has not been healed.

We live in a time when it's popular to blame everyone else for our problems. It's someone else's fault if we are not happy or if we fail at something. If we get a speeding ticket, it's a speed trap. If we get a bad grade, the teacher is unfair. If someone tries to correct us, they are judgmental.

As a principal, it's always a sad thing when parents will not hold their child responsible for his or her actions. Blame is assigned to "those friends" of his or to the teacher who "picks on him" or the coach who "doesn't like him." The unfortunate thing is that too often, this child grows up without learning to take responsibility. When we hide behind excuses, we can't come to terms with who we are, and consequently, we can't grow.

The second group we want to look at are those who blame themselves for everything that happens. Sometimes these people are harder to deal with than those who blame others.

Several years ago, I got a call from Laura Baker, a wonderful retired lady who lived with her husband on the lake. I sensed desperation in her voice when she asked if I would come and talk with her. When she opened her door, Ms. Baker looked like she had not slept in a week. Her face showed the pain of someone who had lost her best friend.

We sat down in the living room, and she immediately began to share with me her story of sorrow. Laura and her husband had retired to the lake mainly so their grandchildren would have a fun place to come to when they visited. One particular granddaughter came to visit more than the rest and became friends with the daughter of the people next door. The more she visited, the tighter the two girls became. Laura thought the relationship was great until she learned that the girl next door had introduced her granddaughter to drugs. One thing led to another, and Laura's granddaughter was addicted and was sent away for treatment.

Laura blamed herself. "We moved here so we could have a place to share with our grandchildren. If I had known this was going to happen, we would never have come here. It's our fault." Laura had not slept for days and was worrying herself to death. Her guilt was destroying her life from the inside.

Now I must admit that I am somewhat of a worrier myself. My wife would say that is a bit of an understatement. I know what it's like to stay awake at night and worry about the problems of yesterday. Laura and I talked and prayed for much of the afternoon that day. It took some time, but Laura finally began to accept the fact that she was not to blame for this unfortunate situation and that she was not doing anything to help her granddaughter by blaming herself.

One of my pet projects as a principal is to try to intervene when kids say mean things about one another. It starts in kindergarten on the elementary playground. Kids begin to tease and call one another names. The kids who take the brunt of these verbal attacks often begin to think of themselves as failures or "not like everyone else." Their self-esteem plummets and sometimes they go through their entire lives carrying a heavy load of hurt and pain. They end up blaming themselves and live defeated lives. It is a barrier that only the grace of God through Jesus Christ can tear down.

I remember an episode of *The Andy Griffith Show* where Barney and some other local residents of Mayberry start teasing a guy named Henry Bennett. Barney loses a game of checkers and, of course blames, Henry Bennett for looking over his shoulder and breaking his concentration. One thing leads to another, and Henry Bennett becomes known as "the town jinx." What started off as a joke becomes bad enough that Henry is on the verge of leaving Mayberry. The interesting thing is that even Henry starts believing that he's a jinx, especially when Andy takes him fishing and the boat sinks. But good ole Andy comes to the rescue, and with the help of the town, including Barney, Henry's self-esteem is restored. Sometimes society can do a pretty good job of making people think it's all their fault and that life is never going to get better.

Finally, there is a third group. There are those who blame God for every bad thing that happens.

Several years ago, I was cleaning up after an assembly program when I found something that disturbed me. Some Christian flyers had been placed at our school advertising a youth rally for the upcoming weekend. There in the bleachers I found one of the flyers with a lot of inappropriate things written on it by one of our students. What really caught my attention was some profanity that had been written around the word *God*. I was shocked and set out to find the students who had written the graffiti. After some investigating, a young man named Randy sat in my office across from my desk. Randy was one of those students who seemed somewhat isolated from most of the activities at school. Usually dressed in black, he seemed to be into rebelling against the norms of society. While we had a strict dress code, Randy liked to live on fringes of what we allowed at school. While I'm sure that in his eyes, I represented the full extent of the establishment, we seemed to have a pretty good relationship. I've always tried to make a habit of breaking the barriers of those groups in school who are a little isolated from the mainstream, and in this case, it helped me have an open line of communication with Randy.

He admitted to having written the profanity on the flyer. When I questioned him on the part about God, he gave an answer I will never forget. "Mr. Coleman," he said, "when I was five, my father left my mother and I all alone. I have never seen him since that day. It's been tough on my mom trying to make it and be the father that I never had. I guess I've handled that all right, but last year, I found out my mother has cancer. She has already started her treatments. It doesn't seem fair. I really don't think there is a God, but if there is, then I hate Him for what He's done to us."

It was heartbreaking to hear his story. At first, I wanted to tell Randy how God had blessed my life through my family, but then I knew that would probably only make things worse. In my heart, I wondered why I was so lucky and why some like Randy had such a tough time in life. It was easy to understand his outward reaction to life when you saw into his heart and what he was feeling. We had a long, honest talk, more about his life than about his inappropriate conduct. From that day forward, Randy went on the prayer list at our Bible study and in my devotional time. I began to observe him at school more closely than I once did. He was an incredibly gifted student with great potential. Then one day, at a school assembly program, Randy gave his life to Christ. It touched the entire student body to see the change that followed. Randy began to share Christ with others and got involved with a lot of school activities to strengthen his witness. He is a living testimony to how Christ can fill even the deepest voids in our lives.

And then there was Sara, a little girl who attended the church where I was pastor in college. At age nine, while riding her bike, she was struck and killed by a car driven by a drunk driver. Just like that, the little girl who hugged my neck every Sunday after church was gone. I'll never forget sitting at the kitchen table with her mom when the question came, "Billy, why did God have to take Sara?"

I was twenty-one years old then. I'm forty-seven now, and I still don't have the answers to why things happen like they do. I can tell you that I don't believe God gives kids' moms cancer, and I don't believe He makes a drunk driver run over little girls. What I do believe and know is that God will use those situations to reach others and to let us all know that we are not alone, which brings us to Jesus's response to the disciple's question, "Master, who's to blame?"

Jesus's response to the disciple's question is twofold. Number 1 is His verbal response: "Neither is to blame." Number 2, and most importantly, is what He did. *He made the man where he could see!*

In other words, Jesus was saying it's not important whose fault it is. To be sure, there are consequences in my life due to my poor choices; these are certainly my fault. On the other hand, sometimes, things happen that are out of our control. The good news is that it does not matter whose fault it is—*Jesus came to fix it.*

The entire ninth chapter of John is devoted to the man who was born blind—the whole chapter! Jesus approaches the man and spits on the ground to make mud. This in and of itself was in violation of Jewish law. It was the Sabbath, and the law said you could spit on a rock, but you could not spit on the dirt because this would make mud and constitute working on the Sabbath. Jesus certainly was sending a clear message to those who worshipped the law. Earlier in this chapter, I mentioned that the law always had to have someone to blame. But God's grace leaves no one to blame. It is a free gift. It is unconditional. If Jesus can use His spit to make a difference, what can He do with our lives!

Jesus rubbed the mud on the man's eyes and commanded him to go and wash it away in the pool of Siloam. The man did what Jesus asked and went home seeing. Then the questions started. First his neighbors, then the Pharisees begin to drill the man to find out how this miracle occurred. Not satisfied, they turn to his parents, who quickly reminded them that he "is of age and will speak for himself." We are told that his parents were afraid of the Pharisees.

The Pharisees return to the man once again to ask the same questions. I love the man's reply this time. "Why do you want to hear it again? Do you want to become His disciples too?" The Pharisees angrily hurl insults at him and eventually throw him out of the temple.

Jesus hears what has happened to the man and finds him. Think about that for a moment. Jesus seeks the man out because there is still a need in his life. Jesus is not finished with him yet, and He seeks the man out. He says, "Do you believe in the Son of Man?"

"Who is he, sir?" the man asked. "Tell me so I may believe in Him."

Jesus said, "You have now seen him. In fact, he is the one speaking with you."

Then the man said, "Lord, I believe," and he worshiped Him.

What a powerful chapter! It does not matter who's to blame, whose fault it is. It does not matter how wrong you are or how many mistakes I make. Jesus came to fix it. All He wants is our okay to proceed.

Jesus is the great fixer. A lady caught in the act of adultery—everyone pointing their fingers at her and blaming her—and Jesus says, "Go and sin no more."

A crowd needing to be fed, a man with a withered hand, a thief on a cross... Jesus came to fix it.

An emptiness in your heart, a failure in my life, a loneliness in our soul, the sins of our past... Jesus came to fix it.

Most of all, He calls us to be His instruments to fix the emptiness and darkness of the world. He calls you and me to answer the question, What are we going to do about it?

The problem with blaming is that it does not solve anything. After you've figured out whose fault it is, you still have a multitude of problems. The disciples could have had a lengthy debate on who was to blame for the man being born blind. But when they finished their discussion, you know what? They still had a blind man in need of a savior.

I remember how important this chapter became in my life when West Point High School burned down. There was the temptation to focus on those who had brought about that great tragedy and how they should be punished and how pitied we were to be for having to suffer such a loss. But who was going to fix it? Who was going to provide school for 550 teenagers? Reality is that all our blaming does not help solve the problem, and our real focus has to be what are we going to do about it. This is the "call to live" that Christ challenges us with.

When I think about the fixing power of Christ, I think about my friend George. As I have mentioned, I was pastor of a church when I was in college. In our little community lived a man named George who was a victim of the disease we call alcoholism. No one could remember ever seeing or talking to George when he was not under the effects of alcohol. Each day I watched him pass as he drove to the local town to buy his liquor. At that time, I did not know him personally but ran into him from time to time in the community. Always there were the red eyes and the heavy alcohol breath. George had been drinking for so many years that it was simply a way of life. His wife and children had long left him to live alone with his disease.

One Sunday morning, out of the clear blue, George showed up at our worship service—in his usual state. Realizing that the roof did not fall in as expected, a sense of awe and expectation began to run through the entire congregation. The first visit was followed by another, then another, with each time George appearing to be a little less intoxicated. On his fourth Sunday, George came down to the altar, looked at me, and said, "Baptize me!" I simply did what he asked, and George accepted Christ into his life.

The following Sunday, George joined the church. It was indeed a wonderful experience. After the service, I noticed he was going around the sanctuary, gathering up bulletins. When I inquired about it, George said he wanted to mail bulletins to all his family so they would believe that he had changed his life! So began the recreation of a new creation in Christ.

The next day, George showed up at the parsonage with his painting equipment. He was a painter by trade, and he had come to paint the whole house, inside and out. He faithfully attended all our Sunday services. He was always there on Wednesday night. He never touched another drop of alcohol. Each spring, George hosted an Easter egg hunt for all the children in the community. It was something everyone looked forward to. George was a committed servant of Christ for the next eight years until he died of cancer. I was coaching by then but had the blessing of speaking at his funeral. It was a celebration of his eternal life with Christ. You know, even eight years later, there were many members of his family who did not attend his services. They still could not believe that it was possible for George to have changed. I thank God for George's life, and as long as I have the opportunity to speak for Christ, I will tell his story. Mistakes and failures condemn us under the law, but the grace of God saves us. While we can't change the past, the grace of God through Christ can *erase* it. Jesus came to fix it.

One of my favorite times in church used to be "the greatest in the kingdom class" where all the children would come down for a short lesson. I admit that sometimes they would catch me off guard, but most of the time, they revealed the truth in the way it was meant to be.

My favorite children's lesson was taking a piece of paper and letting volunteers tear it in several places. Then together, we try to fix the paper. I pull out tape and tacks and gym clips to try to make the paper back the way it was. The kids watch me as I try to fix holes and tears unsuccessfully. When we finish, we have a pretty ugly piece of paper, not good for much of anything. Then we begin talking about how Christ fixes our lives. I pull out a new sheet of paper, and we replace the old with the new. That's what Christ does with our lives. He erases the scars. He forgets the failures. He forgives the sins. He fixes our lives by replacing the old with the new.

Jesus did not come to blame. He came to fix it.

What are we called to do?

The Man in the Hole in the Middle of Town

Once a man fell into a hole in the middle of town. Tried as he could, he simple could not get out.

A coach came by and was later heard telling his team, "Let's win one for the man in the hole."

A teacher came by and told the man five ways people fall into holes and seven ways one can avoid doing so.

A principal came by and asked the man what he was doing so close to the hole.

A preacher came by and preached quite a good sermon on how sin causes us to fall into holes.

A Sunday school teacher came by and asked him if he could attend church as soon as he got out of the hole.

A counselor came by and asked him exactly how he fell in and explained how others had fallen into holes.

A choir director came by and dedicated the anthem that Sunday to the man in the hole.

A lawyer came by and asked the man whose hole it was and explained his legal options.

A doctor came by and lowered a prescription and a bill into the hole.

A nurse came by and provided medicine and bandages.

A politician came by and told the man he had voted not to put the hole where it was and that he would try to get money to fix the hole.

A councilman came by and suggested putting up a sign to warn people of the hole.

A committee chairman came by and took some notes. Soon there were shrubs and flowers placed around the hole.

A mission leader came by and lowered clean clothes and food down into the hole.

One day, Jesus came by, reached down His hand, and pulled the man out of the hole. Then the two of them walked off into eternity together.

Being a Priest

CHAPTER 8

———◦❮❖❯◦———

Being a Priest

> But you are a chosen generation, a royal
> priesthood, a holy nation, His own special
> people, that you may proclaim the praises of
> Him who called you out of darkness into His
> marvelous light; who once were not a people
> but are now the people of God, who had not
> obtained mercy but now have obtained mercy.
> —1 Peter 2:9–10

I know what you're thinking. "Me, a priest? You've got to be kidding. A Christian, for sure. A witness, hopefully. A servant…sometimes. But a priest? I have a wife. I like to eat. I don't pray enough. I like to talk. I just don't measure up!"

Before you skip over to the next chapter, give me the chance to explain. Once again, let's go back to the days of the law. We've already discussed that the law maintained separation between God and man. Man's inability to keep the law made the relationship impossible.

Nowhere was that more evident than the organization of the temple in Jerusalem during Jesus's ministry. Begun in 20 BC, the temple towered fifteen stories high. In the outermost area, there was a huge courtyard, where Gentiles were allowed to go. Beyond that, there was an inner courtyard for the Jews where the praying wall was located. There they could pray but could go no farther. Only the priest could enter the inner area of the temple, called the Holy Place. Furthermore, only the High Priest could enter the Most Holy Place, the area where God resided. A huge curtain separated the Most Holy Place from the rest of humanity. It was there that the high priest would make the blood sacrifices to God on behalf of the people in hope that God would forgive them of their sins.

What we need to remember is that ordinary Jews and no Gentiles were allowed into the holy areas of the temple. That was reserved for the priest, and therefore, it was the priest who represented God to the people, and only the high priest could enter the presence of God. During Jesus's day, that high priest was Caiaphas, a man we are very familiar with during the crucifixion. Jesus's words to Caiaphas and the other religious leader were stinging, and Caiaphas wanted Jesus dead. His motives and actions were not those of a man who spent his time in the presence of God. In reality, Caiaphas was no closer to God than any other man. His sins separated himself from God just like everyone else.

But one day, something happened in the temple that would forever change the relationship between God and man. When Jesus died on the cross, when the sky turned dark, when the spotless Lamb was slain, the curtain that set apart the Most Holy Place was torn. It was torn right down the middle! The place where God lived was opened up to everyone. No more praying wall. No more Holy Place. The physical objects of faith were replaced with spiritual ones. The Most Holy Place became the heart of every believer. God no longer lived behind a curtain! God's presence was available to everyone through the death of His only Son, Jesus Christ! We became reconciled to the Father through the Son!

When that happened, you... I...everyone who believes in Christ became a priest. The ninth chapter of Hebrews says, "Jesus became the high priest." He became our advocate to the Father. And through Him we became priests!

A priest is anyone who believes in Jesus Christ as Lord and who represents God to the world!

Now let me point out how much respect I have for those who have chosen to follow the vocation of priesthood. For so long, that's what I thought of when I thought of a priest: someone who lives in a monastery and is totally devoted to God. I have always admired their discipline and their obedience.

Oh no, I said the word, didn't I? I said the word...*obedience.* You thought we were going to get through the whole book without saying the "O" word. All this good talk about grace and how it's impossible to measure up to the law, and now I have to ruin it by bringing up the thing about "obedience."

And therein lays the problem. Too often we think of obedience like a twenty-five-pound weight around our neck. Rules and regulations—dos and don'ts of Christianity take all the fun out of life, don't they? That seems to be what the world thinks when it looks at the Christian. Do you suppose we have given the world that impression? The truth is that obedience should be a joy and should encompass all the things we really enjoy doing.

When I speak of obedience, please don't think I'm talking about some performance-based Christianity that runs parallel to the Jewish law. It is not a series of actions that we feel like we have to do or are obligated to do. Let me emphasize that the key to obedience is not discipline. The key to the joy of obedience is love.

As a football coach, if you had asked me what is the key to a successful football program, I would have almost knocked you down with the answer, "Discipline, of course!" After all, you've got to have discipline if you're going to make it during those hot all-day practices in August. You've got to have discipline if you are going to be able to win the fourth quarter when the game is on the line. You've got to have discipline when your buddies want you to go fishing instead of attending summer workouts. Yes, I would have answered "discipline." And I would have been wrong!

While I still believe discipline is very important to a successful football program, I now believe that another foundation is more important. Even more important than discipline, I think "love of the game" is the real foundation of a great football program.

Think about it for a minute..."love of the game." You see, you can discipline players and make them go through the difficulties of football. You can probably make them run and sweat. You might get them to make sacrifices. But it is really hard to make them love the game.

On the other hand, show me a player who really loves the game, and I'll show you a player who is willing to work and make sacrifices, who will give all he has in the fourth quarter, who will do whatever it takes. Why? Because he loves the game of football. He *loves* the game. And he will do anything he needs to do to be the best he can be. I've coached guys like that. You cannot work them hard enough. They won't leave the field house after practice. They are always asking you for the keys to the weight room so they can put in extra time. The rigors of football are a joy to them. They love the game!

In the communion liturgy used on the Emmaus Walk, the expression used in one of the prayers to God says, "Free us for joyful obedience." I love that phrase. When we experience the love of Christ in our lives, we are freed from the drudgery of following the rules. Being obedient is something we want to do.

So the key to the joy of obedience is love. Jesus said, "If you love me, you will keep my commandments." If we are struggling with the "O" word...if being faithful is "dragging" us down...we don't need more discipline. We need more love.

I learned that from my good friend in Christ, Adrian Despres. Adrian is a six-foot-six man of God who played football at Furman University and now speaks all over the country to young people for Christ. I first heard Adrian at a national camp for the Fellowship of Christian Athletes and then had the pleasure of hosting him as he spoke at a local youth rally and at West Point High School.

Adrian shared about how he accepted Christ on a night while still in college. He arrived at his dorm room after a "night on the town," only to find his roommate reading the Bible. Adrian confessed his sins and accepted Christ while in bed that night. The next day, he read the book of Matthew. By the end of the week, he had read the entire New Testament.

Sunday morning came, and as was the habit in the athletic dorm, everyone was sleeping in...everyone except Adrian. He got up to go to church and, after some highly persuasive conversation, soon had all his "lineman pals" in the car to go to church with him.

Listen to Adrian's words as he describes that Sunday visit. "I love watching great athletes play sports, and I always like to get as close as I can to the action. This time, I was going to worship the Creator of these athletes, so I wanted to sit on the front row. I didn't know you weren't supposed to sit there. We all walked down front and sat on the front row because it was wide open and gave us plenty of room to sprawl out. We started to sing some songs. I didn't know the tunes real well, but the words were pretty cool. And then the guy starts preaching and was preaching on the New Testament. I had just read some of that stuff, and it was awesome! I thought, 'Wow, is that what that means?' I mean, it was great! I probably should not have turned around and looked behind me, though, because I saw two evil things. Number one, I saw people actually dozing off and going to sleep. I could not believe it. And then I saw what is the worst thing on the whole planet. I actually saw people looking at their watches like they were kind of ready to go, or they didn't want to stay too long. And I started to cry, and I asked myself, 'What has happened to the church?'"

When someone comes along and desperately falls in love with Christ, he reminds the rest of us that we need to return to our first love: that love we had when we first accepted Christ. That was the message to one of the churches in the book of Revelation. The church in Ephesus had been faithful and had endured many trials, yet Revelation 2:4 says, "Yet I hold this against you: You have forsaken your first love. Remember the height from which you have fallen. Repent, and do the things you did at first."

Do you remember how it was when you first accepted Christ? Remember the enthusiasm, the joy, and the awakening in your life? Complacency will try to replace that first love and destroy it. How easy it is to fall into a spiritual rut and gradually lose "the joy of your salvation."

Obedience is a joy, and it is the strength of a priest when it is founded on Christ's love. "If you love me, you will keep my commandments."

I think about Adrian's story and wonder if we make that kind of impression on others at church, what kind of impression are we making in the world? A priest is to represent God to the world. While words are certainly important in our witness, actions are much more important. Whether we like it or not, the world makes conclusions about Jesus Christ based on the way we Christians live.

One of the most impressionable conversations I ever had was with a young man named Jeff. Now Jeff had been very close to accepting Christ several times in his life but always seemed to draw back before making the decision. We had a very open relationship and could talk very honestly about all different aspects of his life, including the spiritual ones. There were a lot of people praying for Jeff. He had a real knack with people and was well-liked by almost everyone, but he really needed Christ in his life as we all do. One day, the subject came up about why he could not take that final step. His reply I will forever remember.

"Coach Coleman, I've been to church, lots of times," he said. "I go there because I have a lot of friends that are Christians. I watch them say their prayers and sing their songs. I listen to them talk about how they love the Lord, and I'm sure they do. But on Friday and Saturday night, they go to same parties I go to. They do the same things I do. They talk a lot about being a Christian on Sunday, but they don't live that way on the other days. And when you really get down to it, I always think, 'They are no different than me!'"

Most of the time, I can at least attempt to answer difficult questions young people have. Talking to teenagers has always come easy for me. But I don't have an answer to that one! Sure, I can point out you need to focus on Christ, not on us Christians, when you are evaluating Christianity. I can speak about how Christ will never let you down while people always will. I can share about God's unconditional love for us even when we are not faithful. But when everything has been said that can be said, you still have the truth that Christians should be different. If we are to represent God to the world, if we are to be priests, God should be reflected in every aspect of our lives.

I am concerned that our young people have been watching the lives of us adults too much. We have given them the impression that it is okay to act one way at church, to talk the talk on Sunday, and to completely be another way in the world during the week.

A recent poll showed that the difference between Christian teens who have had premarital sex and non-Christian teens who have had premarital sex to be only 2 percent! What kind of message does that send to a world that watches every step we Christians take and uses our lives to answer spiritual questions?

When an official makes a call that might cost my team the game—when a parent calls and accuses our school of not caring or when someone is critical of me or my family—it is then my witness takes center stage, and the world silently watches to see if being a Christian makes a difference in the way I live and react to those situations.

The early Christians certainly shared their faith to the world through words. But more than that, they lived their faith. It directed how they lived, and it directed how they died. The world saw their example, and many turned to Christ.

I began to realize how important it was and is for me to represent Christ in *every* area of my life. I need to reflect Christ to the officials, to the opposing team and coaches, to the opposing fans. As sports fans, we are not exempt from being a Christian at those events. I need to realize that others are forming opinions about Christ based on how I act in those situations.

I need to reflect Christ in faculty situations, in the classroom, and at principals' meetings. As a Christian, I need to reflect Christ in every circumstance, in every relationship in my life.

We hear a lot about school prayer and how God has been taken out of the schools in America today. Personally, I disagree with that assessment. I think as long as we have Christian students, teachers, and staff people, God will be in schools. As Christians, we are to carry Him wherever we go. I have seen no court decision that prohibits us from *acting* like Christians at school. And in the end, it will be our actions that make the greatest difference for Christ in the world today.

All the bridges man has ever built to get to God have failed. Some have been constructed by millions, others by only a few. They all have one thing in common: they have all fallen. But one day, God built a bridge. He sent His only Son to reach across the great ravine of sin and gave us access to His presence. The bridge was built, and the curtain was torn; we were reconciled with the Father through the Son.

We as priests are called to stand at that wonderful bridge that God built and say to the world, "This is the one. Through Christ, there is a way to the Father. Take this bridge." We tell the world through our words. But more importantly, we tell the world through our "call to live."

Living the Moment

CHAPTER 9

Living the Moment

Behold, now is the accepted time,
now is the day of salvation.
—2 Corinthians 6:2

"I've got that little girl right in my hip pocket."

Those famous words were spoken by Bernard P. Fife in the confines of the Mayberry sheriff's office. Andy explains to an inquisitive Gomer that the statement is "a figure of speech." Little did Barney know that Gomer would accidentally repeat this "figure of speech" to Thelma Lou, the girl who was supposedly in the fine deputy's pocket. Needless to say, things pretty much went downhill at that point for ole Barn.

In this episode of *Andy Griffith*, Thelma Lou uses Gomer to make Barney jealous and hopefully teach him a lesson. The plan works, and Barney comes crawling back to his girl, vowing to never again take her for granted. As is usually the case, Barney reverts back to his old form by the end of the show with the last line being a repeat: "I've got that little girl right in my hip pocket."

Why is it so easy to take people or things for granted? Maybe one answer is that too often we are so focused on the future that we fail to realize the present. We assume that those around us will always be there, and our focus seems to drift toward what we're going to do, what we're going to get, and what we're going to achieve. We're so wrapped up in ourselves and how we can improve our lot in life we fail to "live the moment." We fail to be thankful for what we have. Most importantly, we fail to appreciate the people in our lives. While living in the future or sometimes the past, we sacrifice the present.

Our nation will never forget September 11, 2001. West Point High School watched the events of that day along with the rest of America and the world. That day, we returned to the present, and for a moment, we wondered if what we had was going to be taken away. We forgot about our future plans, our goals of tomorrow. Our sadness and grief for those innocent people replaced our self-centered attitudes. This country once again became "one" as it had before. We became "one" with those brave firemen and policemen, "one" with our government leaders, "one" with our neighbors. Party lines dissolved. Racial barriers fell. Alabamians and New Yorkers became brothers and sisters. We "lived the moment."

West Point High School joined in with the rest of America in a rekindled patriotism that had long been forgotten. We had real and sincere moments of silence where we prayed for the victims of the day. At our next home football game, we had some students strike that famous pose of the firemen raising the American flag. Over four hundred students with candles raised high surrounded that reenactment in the middle of our football field while a quartet sang "God Bless America."

Who won the game that night took on a different perspective in light of what was really important. No one criticized when people gathered for prayer. We looked at our families through different eyes when we returned home from work. Churches were filled to capacity. Everyone wanted to get involved and help a neighbor in need. We realized how we had taken our country and its blessings for granted. We put the future on hold and began to "live the moment."

Our lives will never quite be the same after September 11, yet we still must battle the tendency to take people and things for granted. We pass by our friends and families on our way to do "important things." We fail to recognize the need of a stranger we meet on the road of life. We even take our relationship with Christ for granted at times.

In the second chapter of Luke, we read the story about Mary and Joseph taking Jesus to the temple when he was twelve for the feast of the Passover. Verse 44 states that on their return home, "thinking he was in their company, they went on a day without him." Of course, they found him in the temple, teaching and listening and asking questions. We can only imagine how Jesus must have impressed everyone even at age twelve.

But that phrase, "thinking he was in their company, they went on a day without him," haunts me. Is it possible to take Jesus so much for granted that we would actually go a day without him in our lives and not even know it? The problem is that it happens so gradually, so slowly. It's not like we mean to drift away. We just begin to focus our energy on "other things," and soon we have left the things that were really important. More so, we leave the people in our lives, even the One who gave His life for us so we could go free.

We think back to a time when we felt so close to Christ. What happened? It's like when you have two lines starting at the same point going in slightly different directions. At first the lines don't seem too far apart, but as they continue, the distance between them becomes greater. The further they go, the further apart they become. Our relationship with Christ can become that way. We begin to move in a slightly different direction, but in time, the distance becomes great. Something happens in our lives to make us take a look at where we are, and we wonder how we ever got so far away. It happens when we don't "live the moment," when we concentrate on the future instead of the present.

"Life is what happens to you on your way to do something important." You know, that statement is really true. All my life, I've been on my way to do something I thought was really important. For seventeen years as a football coach, I was on my way to win a lot of football games. For eight years as a principal, I was on my way to lead our high school to new "levels of excellence." What I discovered was that on my way to achieve those lofty goals, I met some wonderful people along the way who forever changed my life. The trip was much more rewarding than the destination. Every time Shireen and I moved into a new community, we did not know one person in that area. We moved because of the job. But in each instance, if you asked us what we remember most about those situations, we would quickly begin to recall the names of lifelong friends we made. Players and students whom we had the pleasure to coach and teach: teachers, coaches, and staff we were able to work with; friends at churches we attended. And in each situation, whether we realized it or not, there was the chance to share Christ with others. Our lives are interwoven with the many friends we have made "along the way."

And God can use "living the moment" to do some pretty remarkable things.

As I have already mentioned, we had a very active Fellowship of Christian Athletes at Benjamin Russell High School. It was my first coaching job, and Shireen and I were about as young as the students. Wesley had not arrived yet, so we pretty much spent all our time in school-related activities. One night at our FCA meeting, it was mentioned that Alexander City, the town where the school was located, needed a Christian place to go for young people: a place that was nondenominational that provided a Christian atmosphere but where any teenager would be able to come and "hang out." Of course, we have all been in these types of meetings where you "talk" about a lot of good projects, but these young people wanted to put their "talk" to action.

Soon an old house was provided in the middle of town, and the renovation project was underway. Cable service and a telephone were provided. Ping-pong tables and other games were donated. Pinball machines were installed, and pretty soon "The Christian Youth Center" was born and opened for the summer. And what a summer it was! There were Bible studies and cookouts, shuffle board tournaments, and a Biblethon that lasted almost seventy-two hours where the entire Bible was read over a speaker without stopping. The youth center was opened every night except Wednesday and Sunday from five o'clock until ten o'clock on weekdays and five o'clock until late on weekends. That eventful summer, attendance at the Christian Youth Center was over twenty-five thousand. I remember one Saturday night, we were going to have a cookout. There were so many kids there I didn't think we had enough hamburger patties. So

I waited before cooking, thinking some would go home. Wrong! At ten o'clock, there were still over two hundred kids present. Somehow, we were able to feed everyone that night. And you thought Jesus only blessed fish and loaves. I'll tell you He can do some pretty neat things with hamburger too!

A lot of kids accepted Christ that summer. All because a group of teenagers decided to "live the moment" and let God do the rest.

Remember the time when Jesus was asking people to follow Him. Several were making excuses, saying they would follow Jesus later as soon as they took care of some other important things. Jesus's response to them was, "Follow me now!" Note the urgency in His words. I love that word *urgency*, the need to get something done right away. We desperately need urgency in our spiritual life. Second Corinthians 6:2 says, "Now is the accepted time."

I remember another time when I was teaching speech at Dora High School. We were brainstorming about different things our class could do in the area of communication. We were talking about some things we could do on the radio when one student said, "What about TV?" One thing led to another, and *Inside Dora High* was born, Alabama's first student-led and student-produced weekly television show.

We found an old storage room crammed so full you could not open the door. We cleaned it out and made a production room. We brought a camcorder from home, and we started filming. The local cable TV station gave us thirty minutes of airtime each week. To say we were not very good at first would be a gross understatement. But in time, we began to improve. We found seven local businesses that became our sponsors, and we made commercials. Soon we purchased some better video equipment and then some editors where we could actually produce the show at school instead of having to go to the TV station. Then the school system built us our own production class-room. *Inside Dora High* went from an idea to a pretty sophisticated show.

I was the head football coach at Dora and, of course, didn't think I had the time to oversee a weekly TV show. I was on my way to do something really important like win some football game. But you know what? When I think back to Dora days, I remember *Inside Dora High* as much as I do the victories on Friday nights. "Life is what happens to you along the way."

Every moment is a chance to live life to its fullest. We should pray that we never take "this moment" for granted.

Jesus was approaching the end of His earthly ministry. He had entered Jerusalem for the last time. He was dealing with the ultimate sacrifice He was being asked to make, and He needed to pray. So He asked three of His most faithful disciples, three of His closest friends, to go with Him. In Matthew, He says to them, "My soul is overwhelmed with sorrow to the point of death. Stay here and keep watch with me." Once again, we sense urgency in His voice. Three times He returns to them. Three times He finds them asleep. At no other point in Jesus's ministry did He need His friends like He did in Gethsemane, yet when Jesus needed them most, Peter, James, and John slept.

You want to run over to them and wake them up. You want to say, "Don't you realize how important this is? How can you possibly sleep at a time like this?" But you see, they didn't realize how important that moment was. The only thing they knew is that they were very tired and that tomorrow would be coming soon. They needed the rest. After all, Jesus would be around tomorrow.

Jesus returned the third time and said, "Look, the hour is near, and the Son of Man is betrayed into the hands of sinners. Rise, let us go! Here comes my betrayer."

How easily Jesus could have looked at those three that night and said, "You are my betrayers. Forget you. You have no idea what I'm about to do for you!" But He didn't. His love was too great for those kinds of words.

There's a great lesson in that story. We never know what each moment holds, the opportunity it presents. What a tragedy it would be to let it pass without really knowing, to be so concerned with ourselves or our future that we pass through it without living it to its fullest.

I love the shepherds in the Christmas story. When the angel brings them the good news about the birth of Christ, what is their response? "Let us go to Bethlehem and see this thing that has happened, which the Lord told us about." You don't hear anything like, "Well, let me find someone to watch the flock so I can go. It's gonna take me a while, but I'll eventually get down there to see that baby." None of that! These shepherds left their sheep, their most sacred possession, and in a way, they left their lives. They "hurried off and found Mary and Joseph, and the baby, who was lying in the manger." Now that's urgency! And were they glad they did! "The shepherds returned, glorifying and praising God for all the things they had heard and seen, which were just as they had been told."

You see, it's one thing to hear about it, but it's another thing entirely to see it, to experience it, to "live it."

When I was in college, one of my favorite couples to visit was Faye and Jeff Holmes. They lived in a small three-room house. There was no car or truck in the driveway because neither drove. One thing you could count on when you went to visit the Holmes was a good feeling and an offer of cornbread and milk. Now cornbread and milk is not my favorite meal, but somehow it tasted better at their house. In fact, everything seemed better at their house. Faye and Jeff were simple people who lived by the world's standards a very simple life, but unlike the world, they seemed very happy. They found joy in the simple things, and they "lived the moment." They found joy in the things I never even thought about.

The movie *Driving Miss Daisy* is about the relationship that develops between a chauffeur and a pretty cantankerous old woman. In that relationship, racial and religious boundaries are erased. At the end of the movie, the chauffeur is visiting Ms. Daisy at the nursing home. She has gotten so feeble she has difficulty feeding herself. The last scene shows a caring old black man feeding a grateful old Jewish lady a piece of Thanksgiving pie. The two of them are "living the moment" as it was meant to be lived.

The illness of my father was ten times more difficult than any other single event in my life. Single children have the opportunity to get very close to their parents, and that certainly was the case with me. My dad and I had shared our lives together in so many ways. His illness was a difficult one that drew to a conclusion in a long hospital stay. It was in those long days at the hospital that God showed me the real meaning of "living the moment." Every moment became precious. Every movement, every glance had meaning. All the things that I thought were so very important sort of disappeared. All that was left was the "moment."

It had been nine days since there had been any response at all from my dad, really weeks since there had been any communication. Still, I was sensitive to each second that passed in that room. It was a Friday night, and I noticed his gaze at me seemed to have some focus in it.

"Daddy?" I asked.

"Yes?" he answered. He seemed to be aware of my presence.

"I sure wish we could go bird hunting one more time."

"I do too," he whispered so low I could barely hear.

I realized that this was a precious moment that gave me the opportunity to ask the question I had thought about the past nine days. "Daddy, are you in any pain?"

"No," came the answer.

"I love you," I said.

"I love you."

Those were the last words my dad spoke on this earth. The following Monday, he went home to God.

I have had a lot of precious moments in my life, but none any more meaningful than those thirty seconds in that hospital room. I thank God that he gave us that moment together and that we were able to "live it" when it came.

It is my prayer that we all take a moment to look around and see what we have not noticed before: the people, the opportunities, and the blessings. We all need to take the time to listen, to eat some cornbread and milk or Thanksgiving pie, to sit in a rocking chair on the front porch and watch a sunset, to smile at a stranger as we go to do something important. Christ is calling us now. Our "call to live" is for the present. Live this very moment to its fullest.

Seventy Times Seven

CHAPTER 10

Seventy Times Seven

> Then Peter came to Him and said, "Lord,
> how oft shall my brother sin against me, and
> I forgive him? Till seven times?" Jesus saith
> unto him, "I say not unto thee, until seven
> times; but, until seventy times seven."
> —Matthew 18:21–22 (KJV)

It seemed like a logical question at the time. Not only logical, it seemed impressive, something that would even impress Jesus. "Lord, how many times shall I forgive my brother when he sins against me? Up to seven times?"

Jesus had been talking about brothers getting along and what to do when one sinned against the other, the steps that needed to be taken. It set Peter to thinking—thinking about certain people, some friends who had done him wrong, people who had laughed or made fun of him, people who had spread lies and rumors about him, people who had cheated him out of what was rightfully his.

Like most of us, Peter found it hard to forgive, especially when these others' "sins" affected his life. It was one thing when someone did something wrong. It was another thing when that something wrong was aimed at him. Jesus talked a lot about forgiveness, so Peter knew that forgiving was expected to some degree. Most of the rabbis Peter had heard speak had always mentioned forgiving someone three times. That in itself seemed hard enough.

Peter could not remember ever forgiving someone three times, but knowing Jesus, just to be on the safe side, Peter decided he would go even further that anyone could expect. He would suggest to Jesus that seven times one should forgive his brother.

Now Peter had stuck his foot in his mouth before, but this time, his words would surely impress Jesus. Why, Jesus would probably brag on him a little like he did the Roman officer and talk about how He had not seen such love and faith in a person in a long time. He might even talk again about how Peter was a rock and how he had the keys to the kingdom. When Jesus had said those things, Peter had never felt such pride and happiness.

Seven times does seem impressive. I remember one popular saying of our time: "Fool me once, shame on you...fool me twice, shame on me." We live in a time when forgiving someone once is a major spiritual feat. Forgiving and forgetting are in the category of a miracle.

The approach we administrators take in school is the more offenses a student has, the more severe the punishment. You might get by with a stern talk the first time, but the more times you break the rule, the deeper in trouble you become. Beyond school, our penal system makes sure repeat offenders are dealt with more severely.

On a personal level, we more closely resemble "an eye for an eye and a tooth for a tooth" mentality. "You got me, but I'm gonna get you back" or "You're not going to take that off him, are you?" or "You just can't let people run over you" or "When are you going to take up for yourself?" These phrases all reflect the ways of the world that we have been raised in.

We cringe a little when Jesus says, "If someone asks you to go a mile, go with him two miles. If someone asks for your coat, give him your shirt. If someone slaps you on the cheek, turn to him the other."

We say, "Lord, are you sure about the cheek thing? Exactly at what point are we to fight back?"

Yes, when you think about it, Peter's statement is very strong. "Lord, how many times shall I forgive my brother when he sins against me? Up to seven times?"

Take a second and think about someone, the same person, doing something really bad to you...*seven times*! Not two times, not three, but seven times. Which of these times would represent the time that you or I would totally disown them as a friend and bring this unfortunate relationship to a quick end? After all, we would say, a person can only take so much!

As impressive as Peter's statement is, Jesus's response leaves us speechless. "I tell you, not seven times but seventy times seven."

"Four hundred and ninety times. Are you kidding me?" We think, "You are talking about the same person doing all that stuff?" What kind of expression do you think Peter had on his face when Jesus said that?

Of course, Jesus knew where Peter was coming from. His words were a dead giveaway. "How many times *shall* I forgive my brother?" Peter might as well have said, "How many times do I *have to* forgive?" or "How many times *must* I forgive?" Peter's emphasis was on works, not on what was in his heart. Peter was still relying on the way of the law to approach his faith. He assumed that the proper number of doings would suffice, with no regard for what the motive of the heart was.

Jesus's answer was not one of arithmetic but one of spirit. We are to forgive our brother *every* time he sins against us. And our forgiveness should be because we want to, not because we have to. Forgiveness is a way of life for the Christian; it is a fruit of the spirit, a product of the vine who is Jesus Christ.

And this capacity to forgive really has nothing to do with what we do. Jesus explains that in the parable that follows His profound response to Peter. He tells a story of a man who has a tremendous debt to a king, ten thousand talents. The king orders the man's family be sold to pay off the debt, but the man pleads for mercy. Filled with compassion, the king forgives the man and lets him go free. This same man having been forgiven found one of his fellow servants who owed him a hundred denarii and had him thrown into prison until the debt could be paid back. When the king heard about this, he found the unforgiving man and had him thrown into prison and tortured until he paid back all he owed. "This is how my heavenly

Father will treat each of you unless you forgive your brother from your heart."

The truth of this story is very clear. *We* are to forgive our brother because *God* has forgiven us by sacrificing His only Son on our behalf. Forgiveness is not about what we do. It is a response to what God has done for us.

I am thankful that God does not keep count of the number of times He has forgiven me. I am quite sure that number would far exceed four hundred and ninety. Our sins were nailed to the cross with Christ. Something else that died there was our unforgiving heart—in its place resides the spirit of Christ, who gives us forgiveness as a fruit of our relationship with Him.

I recall the third verse of one of my favorite songs, "It Is Well with My Soul."

> My sin, oh the bliss of this glorious thought
> My sin, not in part, but the whole
> Is nailed to the cross and I bear it no more
> Praise the Lord, praise the Lord, Oh my soul

Forgiveness is a way of life for a Christian, a way of the heart, the central core of "the call to live."

Bumps on the Road

CHAPTER 11

Bumps on the Road

> My grace is sufficient for you, for my power is
> made perfect in weakness. Therefore I will boast
> all the more gladly about my weaknesses, so that
> Christ's power may rest on me. That is why, for
> Christ's sake, I delight in weaknesses, in insults,
> in hardships, in persecutions, in difficulties.
> For when I am weak, then I am strong.
> —2 Corinthians 12:9

"Lord, it is good for us to be here. If you wish, I will put up three shelters—one for you, one for Moses, and one for Elijah." Those were Peter's words to Jesus as he stood on the mountaintop and witnessed the transfiguration of Christ in all His glory. Jesus's face "shone like the sun, and His clothes became as white as the light." Then Moses and Elijah appeared before them, talking to Jesus.

It's fun to be on the mountaintop. We've all been there at some time in our spiritual journey—those moments when we feel so close to Christ that we get a little taste of heaven itself. Everything seems to be just perfect—we can clearly see the way, and there seems to be no obstacles in our path.

Like Peter—just like Peter—we think, *It is good for us to be here,* and just like Peter, we want to stay forever.

Unfortunately, we have to come down off the mountain. Sometimes we even have to visit the valleys. Maybe that's good, even though we don't want to admit it. The Christian life is not an exemption from difficult situations, stressful circumstances, or even failure.

One of my favorite *Andy Griffith* episodes is about Barney buying his first car from a little old lady named Ms. Lesh. Confident that he had made the deal of a lifetime, Barney loads everyone up for a scenic ride through the country. With Gomer, Aunt Bee, and Opie in the back seat and Andy and Thelma Lou in the front seat, Barney proudly drives off into the sunset: or so it seems.

Not long into the drive, Andy begins to notice some strange sounds coming from the car. Aunt Bee and Thelma Lou say it's just "bumps on the road," but soon Barney realizes that the sounds are indeed not bumps on the road. The fact is that Barney has bought a real lemon from Ms. Lesh, who turns out to be a crook. The scene ends as Thelma Lou steers while everyone else, including Aunt Bee, pushes the car down the road. The one exception is Barney, who is slumped over on the passenger side with a devastated look on his face.

There are and will always be bumps on the road for all of us.

I love to recall the stories of the great wins I have had the pleasure to be a part of. These were moments that made all the hard work and sacrifices seem worth it. But intermingled with those victories were many bumps on the road, representing losses and failures and frustration.

When I was in high school, we played Talladega High School in basketball. It was a powerhouse program in the largest classification in Alabama. On that team were several players who went on and played major college basketball. They had won forty-four county basketball games in a row when they came to visit Sylacauga in 1973. On a cold January night, we were able to upset Talladega by four points. I will never forget that feeling as a player. We were on the very top of the mountain—that is, until we visited Talladega a couple of weeks later, where we quickly plummeted to the valley after taking a good whipping.

That's the way it is in sports—there are mountaintops, and there are bumps on the road. As the *Wide World of Sports* used to say, "The thrill of victory and the agony of defeat."

And that's the way it is sometimes in our faith. Peter probably thought he could stay on the mountaintop with Christ forever, but that was not the plan. One day he was the "solid rock"; the next day he was denying that he ever knew Christ. One day he has the keys to the kingdom; the next day Jesus says to him, "Get behind me, Satan."

Speaking of Satan, I think it's time we realize that he has a plan too. We talk a lot about God's plan, but it's important that we familiarize ourselves with Satan's plan. To be successful in football, it was always important that we scout our opponent to know his tendencies. The same is true about our faith. We need to know that Satan has placed bumps in the road to destroy our faith and undermine our relationship with Christ. We need to understand that there is a spiritual war going on around us, and everything is at stake.

I have already mentioned in an earlier chapter that more than anything, Satan wants our family. I think it is worth repeating. While we're out trying to change the world, he wants to come in through our back door and take over our house. He wants our children, and he wants to come between us as husbands and wives. He knows that if he can get to our children or our spouses, he can destroy us as well as our desire to serve God. I have spent many years in education, and what I have witnessed is an attack on the American family. There is no doubt in my mind that 90 percent of problems we face today in education go back to the home. From every side, the family is attacked. While we are advancing in just about every aspect of our culture, the family seems to be in increasingly greater turmoil.

The first order of business is to return to our homes and kick Satan out. We need to reestablish our relationships with our wives, husbands, and our children.

Another part of Satan's plan is to convince us that our walk with Christ is based on performance of religious dos and do nots. I often think about what my friend Adrian Dupres told me about John 3:16. He said, "John 3:16 scares me to death. You know why? Because of the word *believes*. 'For God so loved the world that He gave His only begotten Son that whosoever *believes* in Him should not perish, but have everlasting life.' Billy, think about that. What does the word *believe* really mean? What if Satan tricks us into thinking that *believe* means something that it's not? That way, Satan wins."

I really hear what Adrian is saying. What if we think that "believe" means an intellectual statement that we believe in God? What if we think that "believe" means simply attending church or some other "performance based" concept of faith? We remember the words of Jesus when He said, "Not everyone who says Lord, Lord, will enter the kingdom of heaven." Satan wins when we go through the motions of being a Christian without truly allowing the risen Christ to come into our life. We must be born again through the grace of God in Christ.

Sometimes it's just too easy in church. It is such a temptation to take things for granted and just let things roll along with no sense of spiritual urgency in our lives. In our complacency, even the most powerful messages can't break those barriers down. And Satan wants us to stay right there. He wants us to think that is what Christians do. It is his greatest lie.

Not all the bumps in the road are placed there by Satan. While it's easy to blame him for all our problems, sometimes we can get into some difficult situations on our own. We make decisions every day— decisions with consequences that accompany each one. It's funny how good my decisions turn out to be when I'm close to Christ and how bad I can mess up when I distance myself from Him.

And sometimes there are bumps on the road when we are trying to live our lives for God to the very best of our ability. We forget sometimes that many of the disciples died martyrs' deaths because of what they believed. Stephen was stoned to death, and Paul had his head cut off—all of them trying to live for Christ. The world will always have bumps on the road if we live for Him. One of His promises was that we would be persecuted for following Him.

I will never forget the first person I visited when I was a nineteen-year-old pastor. I had a lot of enthusiasm and had pretty much decided that I alone would win the whole community for Christ. I pulled up to the first house I came to, got out of my car, and introduced myself as the new pastor to a man sitting on his front porch. I quickly found out that this man attended another church in the community and did not appreciate my visit. I was told with a few choice words that I best not put into print that I was not welcome at his house. I got back into my car with considerable more humility than I had when I arrived. Maybe winning the world for Christ was a little more difficult than I thought. I have never had another visit like that one, and I now realize the important lesson God taught me that day.

The book of Second Corinthians is a letter Paul wrote to a church that had been led astray by some false prophets who followed in Paul's footsteps to sabotage his message. Not only did they preach a different gospel, they attacked Paul personally. They mocked his speaking ability and questioned his faith. Try to imagine Paul's frustration as he writes this letter, trying to defend himself yet not wanting to appear to be boastful. Finally, he decides to use his vulnerability to appeal to these confused Christians. In the twelfth chapter, he speaks of his bump in the road, "To keep me from becoming conceited because of these surpassingly great revelations, there was given me a thorn in my flesh, a messenger of Satan, to torment me. Three times I pleaded with the Lord to take it away from me. But He said to me, 'My grace is sufficient for you, for My power is made perfect in weakness.' Therefore I will boast all the more gladly about my weaknesses, so that Christ's power may rest on me. That is why, for Christ's sake, I delight in weaknesses, in insults, in hardships, in persecutions, in difficulties. For when I am weak, then I am strong."

What a great scripture!

As a coach, I was on the losing side of the scoreboard plenty of times. Most of the time, we were defeated by a team that was better than we were. I remember a particular time when we lost a game to a team we clearly should have beaten. We were better than they were, but on this night, the best team did not win. Those were the losses that hurt me the most—the ones I took personally. That night, I walked into a quiet dressing room. In total silence, sixty players waited on me to "say something that would make it better." It is an awesome feeling to look out at a bunch of guys you love and know that they are counting on you to say the right thing—to know that they trust you completely and that they believe in you. On this particular night, I walked in and stared at them without saying a word. I just did not have anything to say. I left them and walked out behind the field house, knelt behind a gas tank, and began to pray. "Lord, I don't understand. I try to do the right thing. I try to live for you. I feel like I let everybody down. What am I supposed to do?"

As clearly as I've ever heard the spirit of God speak to me came the answer. "My grace is sufficient for you. You don't have to win any games. All you need is me."

God's grace is enough! His grace is enough to take all my faults and failures and use them for His glory. I realized that the problem was not winning and losing; it was who was in control.

I went back into the dressing room where the players were still waiting in silence. I really don't remember what I said. What I do know is that I've never had those kinds of doubts since that night.

There are still bumps in the road. There always will be. But in our weaknesses, God's power is made perfect. At Jesus's weakest moment, when He was sacrificed for our sins, you and I were saved; the sins of the world were forgiven. And at our weakest moments, God will speak the strongest. The bumps on the road will be used for His glory if we only trust and believe.

The Great Easter Bunny Massacre

Be very careful what you say. Be *very* careful what you say. Someone is listening.

The Pastor Pals was a group of preschool children I had the pleasure of working with at church when I was in college. Most of the children were from families who belonged to the church, but some were from families in the community who either attended other churches or did not attend at all. I guess for some parents, it was a babysitting service of sorts, but for most, it was a chance for the boys and girls to do fun things together with the naive young pastor.

They ranged in ages from three to five, and there were a bunch of them. Every Monday, we would meet at the church from 1:00 until 4:00 in the afternoon. Sometimes we would do activities at the church. Sometimes we would go places that usually resulted in unique experiences.

I remember taking the group fishing one time at a local pond. Out of fear for loss of life, I had to make a rule that you could not swing your pole out of the water unless I was there to help you. Sometimes there were seven or eight poles held by multiple children with a fish hanging in the air as the excited fishermen called to me to come immediately and get their fish off the hook. Sometimes there were ten poles that needed to be baited. You get the picture—total chaos!

Another time, we loaded up in a cargo van lined with carpet and went to the movies. Thirty-five little angels came pouring out of the van and lined up to get tickets. The lady at the ticket window let us all in free out of sympathy for me. I think she wondered what I had done to deserve such grueling community service.

Still another time we went to Birmingham to see Vulcan, the great iron man who gazes over the city. Coming down the concrete ramp that led to the statue, I spilled a five-gallon bucket of grape Kool-Aid, which almost washed away a couple of older ladies in front of us. Needless to say, each Monday afternoon, expect the unexpected.

One particular day stands out above the rest. We were all sitting on the front steps of the church, waiting for moms to arrive and carry the Pastor Pals home. It was a couple of weeks before Easter, and the weather was beautiful.

One of the little boys cried, "Look!" As we all gazed to our right, a little half-grown rabbit quietly hopped out from the side of the church and began to eat some grass. Pretty soon we were all gathered on the edge of the porch, watching the rabbit. The kids were all excited but knew to be quiet so as not to frighten our visitor.

Knowing this was the perfect time for a little talk, I began. "You know what, boys and girls, I bet that's the Easter Bunny. He's come to visit you."

"Yeah, yeah, it's the Easter Bunny," several replied.

"That's right," I continued. "He has come to see if you have been good boys and girls. He wants to know if he should come see you this Easter. Have you been good?"

"I've been good," said Tim.

"I've been good," said Mary.

One by one, the Pastor Pals began to share how good they had been and how deserving they were for a special visit from the Easter Bunny. I had those kids eating out of the palm of my hand. I think I could have convinced them that I myself had arranged this special visit. It was a magical moment.

Then came a little bump in the road. About the time I was thinking how brilliant I was and what an expert on childhood I had grown to be, a beagle dog came running out from the side of the church, *grabbed the Easter Bunny*, and made off into the bush with our special guest. There was a shaking process that occurred I prefer not to get into.

Mass hysteria would be considered a mild expression when trying to explain what followed. "Screaming and gnashing of teeth" is a biblical term that comes to mind.

"*The Easter Bunny is dead!*" one little boy screamed as he ran across the steps. Others quickly followed suit.

About that time, the first mom drove up into the parking lot to pick up her Pastor Pal. The child ran to the car, sobbing "Mommy, the Easter Bunny's dead. A dog just ate him." As she looked at me on the church porch, I managed a weak smile on my extremely pale face.

I wonder if any of those kids are in psychological facilities today. Hopefully not, but it seems like a reasonable possibility.

Be assured that the next week at Pastor Pals, we had a very well prepared lesson on the resurrection!

Never Too Late

CHAPTER 12

---◦◦◦---

Never Too Late

Then he said, "Jesus, remember me when
you come into your kingdom." Jesus
answered him, "I tell you the truth, today
you will be with me in paradise."
—Luke 23:42–43

It was almost over. In many ways, maybe he was glad. The thief on the cross beside Jesus surely began to reflect on his miserable situation as anyone would do. His life began to flash through his mind, interrupted only by the intense moments of pain. Not just physical pain—emotional pain, spiritual pain: the result of a life filled with emptiness and sin.

Through my years in education, I have seen many young people whose actions were so miscalculated that one would be tempted to conclude they were "bad" or "evil." But in every one of these lives, there was a past, and in that past were the answers to the questions we all asked. We can never truly understand someone until we understand what he or she has been through and where they've come from. I can't believe this was any different from the thief on the cross. We can only speculate about his past.

Maybe he came from an abused home, where the norm was violence and cruelty—where there was no love, only hate.

Maybe his father or mother was an alcoholic, blinded to their responsibilities by a disease that destroys the fabric of the family.

Maybe he came from poverty so great that stealing was a way to survive in a world that would let you starve. Younger brothers and sisters had to be fed. Work was hard to be found, and when it was, wages were not enough. Stealing became a way of life.

Maybe he was afflicted with a physical deformity that made him the object of ridicule—the kind of kid others seek out and dominate as they try to assure themselves of normalcy. Perhaps he had a sickness that placed him at a severe disadvantage from the beginning, and others were determined to keep him there.

Maybe he got mixed in with the wrong crowd. Desperate for love and acceptance, he would do anything to be part of a group, even if it meant stealing or breaking other laws. He might have become dependent on drugs and needed to supply his habit.

Maybe he was let down by an adult he admired like a teacher and became sour on life when he discovered the adults he looked up to did not practice what they preached. Maybe he became disillusioned with the established religion of the day when he saw the hypocrisy of the so-called religious leaders.

Maybe his skin or nationality was different from the majority. Perhaps he was a Samaritan or some other lower-class individual, and he simply became what others expected of him.

Maybe sin itself took hold of his life with its lies and deceptions and destroyed him before he could realize it.

We will never know about his past, only that his lifestyle took him to the cross beside the Son of God.

Occasionally he would glance over at the One who was beside Him. Jesus seemed much weaker than he or the other. There was a crown of thorns pushed far down on His head. A large crowd had gathered to watch Him die. They screamed and hurled obscenities at Jesus. Mark's account says, "Those crucified with Him also heaped insults on him," so maybe even this thief mocked Christ.

But something happened in the waning moments of this man's life. Maybe he had heard Jesus speak sometime in the past. Maybe it was something he saw in Jesus's eyes at that very moment. Maybe it was when Jesus looked at those very people who thirsted for His death and said, "Father, forgive them, for they know not what they do." Whatever it was, something inside this thief began to grow, and that something was hope.

It didn't make sense. It was too late for him. He had lived a life full of sin and had turned away from every opportunity to follow the law. He had treated his fellow man with hate and indifference. It was crazy. There was no hope for him.

Once again, he looked over at Jesus. He was drawn to him by something he could not explain. Here in this most difficult of all situations, he saw peace in the eyes of Christ—peace like he had never experienced.

From the other side of Jesus rang out the words of the other criminal, "Aren't you the Christ? Save yourself and us." Little did this man know what a great truth he spoke. Indeed, Jesus could not save Himself and us. One had to be sacrificed so the other could be spared. He had to die on the cross to save us. He had to die so we could live.

The thief answered the other, "Don't you fear God since you are under the same sentence? We are punished justly, for we are getting what our deeds deserve. But this man has done nothing wrong." He finally mustered up enough courage to ask the unimaginable. "Jesus, remember me when you come into your kingdom."

And then the answer came…the most beautiful words the man had ever heard, "*I tell you the truth. Today you will be with me in paradise.*"

Grace unspeakable and full of glory…amazing grace…grace, grace, marvelous grace…grace that is greater than all our sin.

That thief on the cross—that one who had never done an act of goodness, that one who had never bore any fruit, that one who had never kept the law—that thief was saved by the grace of God through Jesus Christ! And God has used that thief to bring hope to millions of souls through the ages—souls who thought they did not have a chance, souls who thought they could never be good enough…the "losers" of the world…the "least of these." God has used that thief on the cross to change the world, and he never did anything except ask.

Is there any greater example to the world that it is through grace we are saved, not by works, "lest any man should boast"?

When I think about that thief and what God did through him, I think what God can do through any one of us. I think about how God used a rich friend of mine who accepted Christ very late in his life. I think about how God used an alcoholic friend when everyone else had given up on him. I think about how God used a little nine-year-old girl who tragically died in an accident. I think about how God used a friend who died with cancer. I think about how God used the last moments of a father's life.

With Jesus Christ, it's never too late to receive His grace. It's never too late to accept the "call to live"!

Grace Extension Ministries

Grace Extension Ministries has one purpose: to glorying Jesus Christ through the spoken and written Word. Billy Coleman began speaking at sixteen and has shared all his life to many churches, educational groups, civic organizations, and corporate functions as an inspirational and motivational speaker. As an educator, he served young people as a teacher, coach, principal, and superintendent of education. In Alabama, he was named Coach of the Year in Cullman and Walker Counties and selection to the Sports Hall of Fame in Cullman County. He was named Administrator of the Year in 1997 while at West Point High School and nominated for Superintendent of the Year in Alabama while at Cullman County in 2011. He has spoken at the Governor's Prayer Breakfast and led the National Coaches Bible Study at Black Mountain, North Carolina, for the Fellowship of Christian Athletes.

We invite you to contact Billy at www.graceextensionministies. com if you would like Billy to come and speak or read his devotionals. You can also purchase copies of *Called to Live*.

From Billy,

Thank you for being led to read *Called to Live*. We thank God for your life and pray God will use your life to build a bridge so that Christ can walk into the life of another. May God's peace and grace give you the assurance that we are all one in Christ and all "called to live" for His glory.

In Christ,
Billy

"I must decrease and Christ must increase"
(John 3:30).

ABOUT THE AUTHOR

Billy Coleman has served Christ his entire life as an athlete, a teacher, a coach, a principal, and a superintendent of education. He began speaking to groups at sixteen and, for almost fifty years, has spoken to churches and youth groups, in educational settings, and to civic and professional organizations as a motivational speaker. In college, he was selected as one of three "Outstanding Young Religious Leaders" in Alabama while pastoring a church. He has received "Coach of the Year" honors in Cullman and Walker Counties in Alabama was inducted into the Cullman County Sports Hall of Fame. As principal of West Point High School, Billy was selected as "Administrator of the Year" in Alabama and later nominated for "Superintendent of the Year" as superintendent of Cullman County schools. He has been very active in the Fellowship of Christian Athletes all his life and led the National Coaches' Bible Study at Black Mountain, North Carolina, for FCA. Billy presently lives in Alexander City, Alabama, with his wife, Shireen, and close to their two sons, two daughters-in-law, and four grandchildren. Presently, he leads a nondenominational men's Bible study called Legacy Builders.